T0323624

Cambridge Elements ≡

Elements in Political Psychology
edited by
Yanna Krupnikov
University of Michigan

IN DEFENSE OF IDEOLOGY

Reexamining the Role of Ideology in the American Electorate

Elizabeth N. Simas
University of Houston

CAMBRIDGE
UNIVERSITY PRESS

Shaftesbury Road, Cambridge CB2 8EA, United Kingdom

One Liberty Plaza, 20th Floor, New York, NY 10006, USA

477 Williamstown Road, Port Melbourne, VIC 3207, Australia

314–321, 3rd Floor, Plot 3, Splendor Forum, Jasola District Centre, New Delhi – 110025, India

103 Penang Road, #05–06/07, Visioncrest Commercial, Singapore 238467

Cambridge University Press is part of Cambridge University Press & Assessment, a department of the University of Cambridge.

We share the University's mission to contribute to society through the pursuit of education, learning and research at the highest international levels of excellence.

www.cambridge.org
Information on this title: www.cambridge.org/9781009228176

DOI: 10.1017/9781009228169

First published 2023

A catalogue record for this publication is available from the British Library.

ISBN 978-1-009-22817-6 Paperback
ISSN 2633-3554 (online)
ISSN 2633-3546 (print)

Additional resources for this publication at www.cambridge.org/simas

In Defense of Ideology

Reexamining the Role of Ideology in the American Electorate

Elements in Political Psychology

DOI: 10.1017/9781009228169
First published online: April 2023

Elizabeth N. Simas
University of Houston
Author for correspondence: Elizabeth N. Simas, ensimas@uh.edu

Abstract: Years of collective political science research has fueled the stereotype of the uninformed or illogical American voter who ardently supports parties or candidates but lacks any cohesive ideological reasons for doing so. Prior works, however, do not tell the whole story nor fully capture the nature of public opinion in today's increasingly polarized political environment. Thus, this Element makes the case for more careful and nuanced assessments of ideological thinking in the American electorate. Using a variety of more contemporary survey and experimental data, it shows that a substantial portion of Americans do hold coherent political beliefs and that these beliefs have important consequences for the American political system. Though partisanship still plays a powerful role, the electorate as this Element presents it is much more ideological than the literature too often assumes.

Keywords: ideology, policy preferences, public opinion, voting behavior, polarization

ISBNs: 9781009228176 (PB), 9781009228169 (OC)
ISSNs: 2633-3554 (online), 2633-3546 (print)

Contents

A further Online Appendix can be accessed at
www.cambridge.org/simas

1 Reopening the Argument

In August of 2016, the late-night show *Jimmy Kimmel Live* aired a segment called "Rock the Quote." For this segment, a camera crew was sent to a Democratic rally to interview individuals who were supporting Hillary Clinton in the 2016 presidential race. Each person featured was read what they were told was a quote from Clinton, and then asked whether or not they agreed with that quote. The gag? All of the quotes were actually from Donald Trump, Clinton's Republican rival for the presidency. The result was a compilation of clips of individuals who were sporting all varieties of pro-Clinton or pro-Democratic clothing and flair, but agreeing with and even justifying positions like "immigration is a privilege" and "let people keep more money in their pockets" – positions that clearly ran counter to the platform being advanced by Clinton and Democrats at that time.

Though this segment was obviously edited to feature the most extreme and comedic examples, it presents American partisan voters just as years of collective political science research suggests that they actually are: individuals who ardently support a party or candidate, but lack any cohesive ideological reasons for doing so. Indeed, in one of the most influential works in the discipline, Philip Converse (1964) argues that the majority of the mass public are ideologically innocent, lacking consistent, logically connected beliefs. Though this work has been challenged and debated in the fifty-plus years since its publication, there is still widespread support for this thesis, with a recent reexamination concluding that there is "no reason to reopen the case. To the contrary, the results fortify the original verdict. By and large, Americans come to politics without ideology in mind" (Kinder and Kalmoe 2017, p. 125).

I, however, do not see existing works as the complete trial, but rather, just the case for the prosecution of ideology. For every individual featured in the *Kimmel* segment, there were undoubtedly several who recognized the discrepancies in the statements and thus, ended up on the cutting room floor. And while scholars have been much more careful to provide a complete and balanced picture, there is still a wealth of evidence that has yet to be fully explored. Thus, my goal here is to offer a defense of ideology as it currently exists in the American public.

My defense is centered on three major claims: (1) the percentage of individuals with coherently connected political beliefs is larger than is often assumed; (2) for many, these policy beliefs are an important part of the way they think about ideological labels; and (3) these policy beliefs have important effects on political behavior that should not be attributed to identity alone. In making these claims, it is important to clarify that I do not take issue with arguments that certain members of the public do not think in an ideological manner. By any measure or standard, one can always find a segment of the population that fits the definition of ideological innocence. But where I believe that there is room for debate is on matters of just how pervasive this innocence really is. That is, my major argument is that when thinking about the various ways in which an individual may be ideological, members of the American public fit these definitions a good deal more than they are typically given credit for.

I begin by briefly summarizing the case against ideology. I start this with a recap of Converse's (1964) original arguments, and then proceed to discuss more recent works as they fit into what I see as the three major claims about ideological innocence that I counter: (1) people do not hold consistent opinions on issues; (2) people do not think ideologically; and (3) ideology is of little political consequence. Finally, I round out this section with a preview of how I will spend the remainder of the Element responding to these three major lines of argument.

1.1 Converse's Claims

Though Converse prefers the term "belief system," he defines it in a manner that is consistent with most conceptions of ideology – a "configuration of ideas and attitudes in which the elements are bound together by some form of constraint or functional interdependence" (Converse 1964, p. 3). In this definition, constraint and interdependence refer to both the ability to successfully predict an individual's position on one issue simply by knowing their position on another and the probability that when there is some kind of change related to opinions on one issue, there are also compensating changes on others. As such, people with coherent belief systems know "what goes with what" and why. And while elite political actors may fit this definition, Converse's main argument is that most people in the general public do not.

Converse attributes this disconnect to the flow of information. According to Converse, the shaping of belief systems "is an act of creative synthesis characteristic of only a miniscule proportion of any population" (Converse 1964, p. 8). These belief systems are then passed onto to the broader public. The transmission of information, however, is imperfect. Just as in a game of telephone, key aspects of the message get lost as it moves down the line from the source. So as belief systems are passed from the elite political actors at the top to those further removed from the political system, important pieces of information about what goes with what, and in particular, why, go missing. The result is a vertical scale with the few true ideologues in the population occupying the top, and the remaining majority filling out various levels of issue constraint at the bottom.

After laying out this theory, Converse presents evidence of this stratified system. Starting with responses to both open- and close-ended questions from interviews conducted in 1956, he divides individuals into five strata or "levels of conceptualization" of the political system. The top stratum is comprised of the ideologues – those who did appear to evaluate policies and political objects in a coherent way. Only 2.5 percent of the full sample and 3.5 percent of voters fall into this stratum. Near ideologues – the second stratum – is slightly larger but still relatively small, as only 9 percent of the full sample and 12 percent voters of fit here. The third stratum – labeled group interest – was the largest. 42 percent of the full sample and 45 percent of voters fell into this category because although their responses did not suggest reliance on an overarching belief system, they did show awareness of how parties may have positive or negative impacts on different social groupings. The distinction between these individuals and their more ideological counterparts lies in the fact that "unless an issue directly concerns their grouping in an obviously rewarding or punishing way . . . they lack the contextual grasp of the system to recognize how they should respond to it" (Converse 1964, p. 15).

The second-largest category was the fourth stratum, which was labeled nature of the times. This somewhat residual category was populated by the 24 percent of the full sample and the 22 percent of voters who invoked some policy considerations but did not meet the standards for classification in higher strata. This leaves the remaining 22.5 percent of the sample and 17 percent of voters to the fifth and lowest stratum – those whose responses show no issue content.

Yet, as Converse acknowledges, this classification system required recall and habitual use of ideological concepts. Even though individuals may not have appeared to actively draw on ideological concepts when asked without special prompting, they may still be able to recognize and attribute meaning to them when those concepts are directly presented. Thus, Converse drew on 1960 reinterviews of the original 1956 sample that asked a series of questions probing whether individuals viewed one party as more liberal or conservative than the other. On the one hand, the categorizations that result from these responses are more optimistic; about 17 percent of respondents fall into the top stratum of recognition and understanding, meaning that they are able to match the parties to their proper ideological labels and show some broad understanding of the terms. But on the other hand, these data still reveal considerable ideological innocence, as 29 percent still fall into the bottom stratum that shows no apparent recognition of the terms.

Even with the different standards for the two classification systems, there is a strong relationship between the two. And both are related to political information, education, and political involvement such that all three decline as one moves from stratum one down to stratum five. These correlations are particularly important for supporting Converse's argument about how and why belief systems are so stratified. In short, the 1956 and 1960 interviews bolster the claim that coherent, ideological belief systems are only observable among a relatively small group of the most informed individuals.

The presentation of these data is complimented by further analyses of the connections between and stability of various issue opinions. Looking at opinions on issues such as employment and military aid, Converse finds that the opinions of congressional candidates are much more correlated than those expressed by members of the general public. Moreover, individuals' issue opinions are likely to change over time. Even though there are only a few years between the first and second interviews, respondents appear to be likely to change their expressed opinions on a range of issues. This instability is especially apparent when compared to individuals' expressed party identification, which is much more consistent across the two interviews.

There is much more detail and discussion in the full seventy-four pages of Converse's work. But the brief summary provided here is hopefully enough to show the foundations of two of the three major arguments that will be rebutted in the later sections of this Element. The stratifications support the claim that most people do not think ideologically, while the low correlations both within and across issues show a lack of consistent opinions. So although the data are now decades old, the basic arguments endure.

1.2 The Current Case against Ideology

A complete review of all of the many works that have come since Converse would require an entire volume all its own. Thus in this subsection, I focus just on those works to which the evidence I will present later most directly responds. In doing so, I organize them as I see them contributing to the three main claims that I intend to refute. Note that inclusion or omission in this brief review is not a reflection of the merit of a work; decisions were made based on a desire for concision and relevance to the arguments advanced in the later sections of this Element.

1.2.1 People Do Not Hold Consistent Opinions on Issues

Converse's (1964) work paints a picture of "a mass public [that] contains significant proportions of people who, for lack of information about a particular dimension of controversy, offer meaningless opinions that vary randomly in direction during repeated trials over time" (p. 49). And although education levels in the United States have risen, more recent analyses suggest there has been little change. Looking at every pair of policy questions featured on the 1972–2012 American National Election Studies (ANES), Kinder and Kalmoe (2017) find an average correlation of only 0.16. The authors acknowledge that consistency does appear to be higher in the later years, though they estimate that the rate of increase is so slight that it would be about 2315 before ordinary citizens resemble political elites.

Some scholars have pushed back at such findings by arguing that an instability of actual attitudes is just one possible explanation for the low correlations between issue positions. These works instead suggest that much of what Converse (1964) observed may be due to measurement error stemming from vagueness in the questions. That is, when asked about agreement with policies, an individual might choose "strongly agree" in one instance and "somewhat agree" in another not because their actual levels of agreement are different, but "simply because of the ambiguity of the question asked or because he is uncertain how strong is 'strongly'" (Achen 1975, p. 1220). Building off this work, Ansolabehere, Rodden, and Snyder (2008) show that averaging multiple responses on the same broad issue area reduces measurement error, reveals a much greater degree of opinion stability, and offers "evidence that even the least sophisticated are not merely 'guessing' when answering issue questions" (p. 226). Studies of elites (Converse and Pierce 1986; Jennings 1992), however, cast doubt on measurement arguments, as they fail to find the same patterns of instability even when using the same exact questions.

Moreover, Freeder, Lenz, and Turney (2019) show that stability still varies by knowledge even after adding more items. Across multiple studies, the authors find that opinion stability is largely limited to those who both know their party's positions on the issues and agree with them. Overall, their evidence suggests that only 20–40 percent of the US public can be classified as having stable issue preferences and implies an "absence of stable views independent of party" (p. 288).

These analyses of survey data are complimented by a number of experimental works. Though generic party cues do not appear to move issue opinions, party leader cues do exert significant effects. For example, Nicholson (2012) finds that when shown the position taken by the opposite party's 2008 presidential candidate, both Democratic and Republican respondents became more likely to express an opposing position. More recently, Barber and Pope (2019) leveraged the fact that Republican President Donald Trump was on the record as having both liberal and conservative opinions on a number of different issues. Although they do not find the same negative partisan effect that Nicholson (2012) did, they do find that Republican respondents can be moved to keep their positions in line with Trump's. That is, Republicans who were told that Trump supported increasing minimum wage to over $10 an hour also expressed support, while Republicans who were told that Trump opposed the increase were more likely to also be in opposition. These results are particularly striking given that the liberal Trump cues did not simply act as a shortcut to help individuals choose the "correct" position given their identification, but rather, they led Republicans to express policy opinions that oppose what should be some of the more fundamental beliefs of their party. Thus, both survey and experimental studies continue to support Converse's (1964) general claims and suggest that the "simple truth is that many citizens behave as partisan loyalists rather than principled ideologues" (p. 53).

1.2.2 People Do Not Think Ideologically

In the years since Converse (1964), there has been a clear trend of increasing ideological polarization at the elite level such that Democrats have become more cohesively and distinctly liberal, while Republicans have become more cohesively and distinctly conservative (e.g. Poole and Rosenthal 1997). These divisions at the elite level appear to have enhanced clarity and understanding among the general public, as individuals are able to place both parties and their candidates on the ideological scale with increasing accuracy (e.g. Hare et al. 2015; Hetherington 2001). Yet, individuals' abilities to utilize the ideological scale to describe their *own* issue positions remains in question. Specifically, Kinder and Kalmoe (2017) highlight the fact that a large portion of the electorate either cannot or will not place themselves on the seven-point liberal-to-conservative scale. Examining ANES data from 1972 to 2012, they find that when confronted with the ideological scale, the most popular options (chosen by 27.5 percent of those surveyed) are "don't know" or "haven't thought much about this." Although the size of this group does decline over the time period studied, it seems that in any given year, about one quarter of individuals simply do not think of themselves in ideological terms.

And even when individuals do select an ideological label, this should not be taken as evidence that they do possess coherent ideology. For one, the most commonly chosen position on the seven-point scale is "moderate," the middle point. In the 1972–2012 dataset, 24.5 percent of all respondents and 33.8 percent of those selecting an ideological label chose this point on the scale. Survey researchers have long debated about the meaning and effects of including a middle option. While some respondents truly fall in the middle of a given scale, others may choose the midpoint because it is easier than expending the mental energy to discern their true positions (e.g. Krosnick 1991) or because it allows them a desirable alternative to admitting that they do not know (Sturgis, Roberts, and Smith 2014). There is a good deal of evidence to suggest that those selecting the midpoint of the ideological scale tend to fall into these latter categories. Indeed, the issue opinions and information levels of those selecting the middle and those choosing "don't know" tend to be almost indistinguishable (Kinder and Kalmoe 2017; Treier and Hillygus 2009). Thus, if moderates are no different than those who fail to place themselves at all, then it seems that a majority of Americans should be regarded as nonideological.

Second, when respondents choose any point on the seven-point scale, they may be doing so for reasons that have nothing to do with their underlying issue preferences. Using the terminology of Ellis and Stimson (2012; see also Popp and Rudolph 2011), our discussion thus far has been focused on *operational ideology*, or ideological identification that is rooted in one's issue preferences. This maps onto the most common uses of the seven-point ideological measure and fits the general assumption that a person classified as liberal (conservative) should have liberal (conservative) opinions on a range of political issues. However, the political science literature lacks a singular definition of ideology (see Gerring 1997) and has actually identified multiple forms of the concept. Notably, prior works demonstrate the existence of *symbolic ideology*,[1] or any ideological identification that stems from affect and/or desires to be associated with or distanced from those various groups or symbols typically connected to ideological labels (e.g. liberals with nonwhites and labor unions, conservatives with the religious and big business).

While the two types of ideology do align in the majority of cases, they are also very often at odds. That is, there are many people who are operationally liberal (conservative) but symbolically conservative (liberal). Estimates of the numbers of these "conflicted" ideologues – those who identify with an ideological label that is at odds with their actual policy beliefs – vary across studies. For example, Popp and Rudolph (2011) classify 12.9 percent of their sample as conflicted liberals and 9.7 percent as conflicted conservatives, while Claassen, Tucker, and Smith (2014) report the same figures to be 1.5 percent and 10.9 percent, respectively. Ellis and Stimson's (2012) examination of 1973–2008 suggests that the percentage of conflicted liberals ranges from 1 to 5 percent, while the percentage of conflicted conservatives ranges from about 15 to 30 percent (see Figure 5.5 on p. 98). But regardless of the exact numbers, the same major takeaway emerges: for a nontrivial proportion of the public, ideology and the terms associated with it have nothing to do with issues.

---

[1] Malka and Lelkes (2010) use the term "ideological identity," while Devine (2015) refers to this as "ideological social identity."

1.2.3 Ideology Is of Little Political Consequence

The evidence discussed in the previous section – particularly the experimental findings about the power of partisan cues – gives rise to questions about whether people's issue positions really impact political choices and behaviors, or whether partisanship and other identities reign supreme. A number of works have shown that individuals do act in a manner consistent with the expectation that voters select the candidate with the most similar policy positions (e.g. Shor and Rogowski 2018; Tomz and van Houweling 2008) and punish those representatives who are out-of-step (Canes-Wrone, Brady, and Cogan 2002). But increasing polarization at the elite level means that for the vast majority of partisans, voting for the candidate who best matches your issue positions also means voting for the candidate from your own party. For example, in my exploration of voting in the 2010 US House elections (Simas 2013), I find that 83.2 percent of partisan voters in my sample both voted for the closest candidate *and* voted for the candidate from their own party. Thus, evidence increasingly suggests that although voters may appear *as if* they are voting for the closest candidate, they may not actually be able to place the candidates on the ideological scale and instead be voting based on criteria that have little to do with ideology (Joesten and Stone 2014; Tausanovitch and Warshaw 2018).

Kinder and Kalmoe (2017) also argue for the relative unimportance of ideology. Their analyses suggest that in presidential elections, only the most engaged voters cast ideological votes. And in House elections, the authors conclude that ideological voting appears to be nearly negligible. Going further, they also use panel data to show that ideological identification has little if any influence on opinions on a large range of issues that includes immigration, gun control, and tax reform. They do find greater evidence of a relationship between ideological identification and opinions about abortion and gay rights, but this is reduced once religiosity and group sentiments are included. In addition, Kinder and Kalmoe (2017) use individuals' assessments of economic conditions to show that partisanship but not ideology biases these important political perceptions in a meaningful way. These various pieces of evidence all lead to the general conclusion that when individuals make important political judgments, ideology is simply not consequential.

There is also little to suggest that belief systems are contributing to increasing levels of hostility. Though scholars continue to debate whether the public is polarized on the issues (e.g. Abramowitz 2011; Fiorina, Abrams, and Pope 2011), there is greater consensus around the idea that partisans in the general public are divided by the animosity they feel for one another (Iyengar, Sood, and Lelkes 2012). This affective polarization is evident in sentiments, biases, and prejudices expressed both in and out of the political realm (e.g. Iyengar and Westwood 2015; Lelkes and Westwood 2017). But when looking at how liberals and conservatives feel about one another, there does not appear to be a similar divide (Kinder and Kalmoe 2017). Mason (2018) does find greater evidence of affective polarization among liberals and conservatives, but she argues that this is driven by identity, not issues. In two different samples, Mason (2018) finds that animosity is greatest among those with the deepest attachments to their ideological labels, regardless of where they stand on the issues. The existence of these "ideologues without issues" adds to the argument that ideology as conceptualized by Converse (1964) has little effect on real-world political outcomes.

1.3 The Need for Reevaluation

While the aforementioned critiques are grounded in sound, peer-reviewed research, I contend that they do not tell the whole story nor fully capture the nature of public opinion in today's increasingly polarized political environment. In the following subsections, I highlight the three main areas that need to be considered when thinking about ideology in the modern electorate.

1.3.1 Both Elites and Voters Have Changed

Even when updating Converse, many scholars have had to rely on panel data from the 1990s or early 2000s. I offer a more updated look at ideology, drawing on wide variety of surveys that were conducted as recently as 2020. A focus on more recent data is particularly important given two major changes in the American political landscape. First, party leaders have staked out increasingly distinct positions across a host of issues. Studies of both legislators (Hare and Poole 2014) and political activists (Collitt and Highton 2021) show clear patterns of polarization at these highest strata. Since Converse's (1964) argument is so dependent on the top-down flow of information, this suggests that changes at the high levels should lead to changes for those levels below. Though the transmission of information is an imperfect process, clearer signals from the top should reduce at least some of the distortion that occurs further down the line.

Second, though ideological thinking may be limited to the most informed, levels of education[2] and political information are both on the rise. For example,

---

[2] www.census.gov/library/stories/2018/07/educational-attainment.html#:~:text=The%20October% 202018%20Current%20Population,population%203%20years%20and%20older.&text=In%20the% 20U.S.%2C%20per%20student,and%20enrollment%20was%2048.6%20million. Accessed June 24, 2021.

the Annenberg Constitution Day Civics Survey shows that between 2006 and 2022, the percentage of US adults who can name all three branches of the government rose from 33 percent to 47 percent.[3] While the fact that less than half of Americans can correctly answer this basic civics question may not be particularly reassuring, the upward trend still suggests the potential for an increase in the number of people with cohesive beliefs. So altogether, my argument is that clearer cues from elites and greater capacity for processing those cues in the general population should increase the overall percentage of individuals with consistent issue opinions.

1.3.2 Ideology Is Not Just an Identity

While some claims about ideological innocence center around a lack of consistency in issue positions, others focus on the facts that many individuals avoid ideological labels or choose labels that do not accurately describe their political beliefs. But mismatches between a person's symbolic and operational ideologies should not automatically be dismissed as a lack of an understanding of how policies map onto the liberal-conservative continuum, and the two conceptions need not align to be meaningful. This is articulated more eloquently by Ellis and Stimson (2012), and further evidenced by the work of Groenendyk, Kimbrough, and Pickup (2022), which makes a clear case for the distinction between awareness of ideological norms and the expression of preferences that are consistent with such knowledge.

And indeed, a growing number of works show that people can and do connect issues to ideological labels in a meaningful way. When presented with vignettes that describe the policy positions of hypothetical individuals, survey respondents were on average able to place them at the intended point on the ideological scale (Simas 2018). Using an experimental approach, Goggin, Henderson, and Theodoridis (2020) find similar results, as both high- and low-knowledge individuals demonstrate an ability to accurately guess a candidate's ideological identification (i.e., either liberal or conservative) based on a list of personal attributes and policy positions. Even more, the authors find that the strength of the policy-to-ideology connection is on par with the connection between policy and partisanship, leading them to conclude that "contemporary voters may grasp more of the ideological conflict in American politics than the voters analyzed by Converse (1964) in the middle of the last century" (Goggin, Henderson, and Theodoridis 2020, pp. 1004–5). So while some individuals may continue to treat to the two conceptions of ideology as distinct, others likely

---

[3] www.annenbergpublicpolicycenter.org/americans-civics-knowledge-drops-on-first-amendment-and-branches-of-government/. Accessed September 28, 2022.

do draw on this increasing grasp of conflict and tie their political beliefs to their identities. Thus, I present a deeper examination of how and why people use the ideological scale and argue that there is indeed evidence of a distinctly issue-based component.

1.3.3 Policy Opinions Operate alongside Partisanship

The vote choice models that Kinder and Kalmoe (2017) present when dismissing the role of ideology actually have two measures of the concept – identification on the seven-point scale and policy views. Together, these two measures represent both the symbolic and operational aspects of ideology. Across the six models, eleven of the twelve coefficients are significant. So while the effects of partisanship are undeniable, these additional variables show that ideology does contribute to our understanding and may be particularly useful for distinguishing between individuals who share the same partisan identification.

The large effects of policy views are also consistent with a growing body of work showing the importance of operational ideology. Individuals are willing to punish co-partisans as disagreement with their policy stances increases (Mummolo, Peterson, and Westwood 2019). And across three different experiments, Costa (2021) finds that when evaluating representatives, individuals prioritize issues over affect, as legislators were rewarded for taking desirable policy positions but not for expressing animosity for the opposite party.

Issue positions also play a powerful role in fueling animosity. Studies looking at individuals' feelings about both elites and ordinary partisans repeatedly find that issue information increases animus beyond what is observed when only partisan identities are known (Clifford 2020; Lelkes 2021; Orr and Huber 2020; Rogowski and Sutherland 2016; Webster and Abramowitz 2017). Though much of the effect of policy is due to the fact that it signals party identification, there is still a substantial independent effect. For example, Dias and Lelkes (2022) report that preferences on issues that are not readily linked to partisanship (e.g. eminent domain, the sale of consumer mobile data) reduced the effects of partisanship by about one-third. And since these "unbranded issues are orthogonal to partisanship, these effects can only be a function of policy disagreement" (Dias and Lelkes 2022, p. 14). Subsequently, I add to evidence of the independent effects of people's policy views.

1.4 Organization of the Element

Given ample reasons to reevaluate ideology in today's electorate, each of the next three sections addresses one of the major lines of criticism of ideology.

In Section 2, I examine the three key pieces of evidence that are most often cited when individuals critique Americans for a lack of meaningful issue positions: (1) the consistency between opinions on different issues; (2) the stability of opinions over time; and (3) the extent to which opinions can be changed by party cues. My analyses all suggest an electorate whose opinions are far from incoherent. First, I show that the correlations between opinions reported on the 2010–2020 Cooperative Election Study (CES) surveys and the 2020 ANES are all substantially greater than those reported by previous works. Second, I use the 2010–2014 CES panel study and the 2016–2020 ANES panel study to show that over time, the opinions of the full samples are just as if not more stable than those of just the most knowledgeable individuals in the samples used by prior studies. Even when I look at those with lower levels of political knowledge or those who do not place themselves on the ideological scale, I find a fair amount of consistency and stability. Finally, I present experimental results that show only a very limited amount of movement in response to party leaders' positions.

In Section 3, I show that people can and do connect issue positions to ideological labels. I begin by using ANES data from 1988–2020 to show that although a large portion of individuals do not initially choose an ideological label, most do when pressed (via a follow-up question that researchers typically ignore) to select either liberal or conservative. Thus, I push back against claims that ideologues are the minority in the United States. Next, I utilize responses to open-ended questions to provide a better picture of what people think about when they use ideological labels. Responses from the 1992 ANES, a proprietary module of the 2018 CES, and an original 2019 Lucid survey all show that thoughts about general philosophy and specific policies outnumber comments about groups or parties. Finally, I raise the possibility that some of the issues with the standard measure of ideology may stem not from the answers that people give, but from the question itself. Using data from my 2018 CES module, I show that a different format of the ideology question elicits responses that are more highly correlated with respondents' actual policy preferences. Moreover, I show that the biggest improvements are among those with little political knowledge or no partisan attachments – two groups often the target of claims of a lack of ideological thinking.

After establishing that people do hold consistent beliefs and that their under-standing of ideological identifications are connected to their beliefs, I turn to showing that ideology is related to important political outcomes. I start Section 4 by looking at voting. Using panel data sets that allow me to model vote choice or vote intention as a function of opinions and characteristics measured at an earlier time period, I examine individuals' (1) 2012 presidential votes; (2) 2012 US House votes; (3) 2014 US House votes; (4) 2018 US House votes; and (5) 2020 presidential vote intentions. In all cases, I show that ideology – whether represented as identification on the ideological scale or as opinions on issues – is a significant predictor of which party an individual chooses to support. I then present experimental evidence that allows me to better isolate the effects of issue positions or operational ideology. These experiments show that issue positions do contribute to partisan animosity.

I conclude this Element with Section 5, which briefly recaps my major findings and discusses both implications and future directions. Altogether, the evidence presented will reinforce the argument that although Americans frequently appear to support or oppose a political side in much the same way that they cheer for or against a football team, there often is a more logical and substantive basis to people's behavior and opinions.

2 Another Look at Issue Attitudes

During the 2010s, there was no shortage of media narratives blaming Millennials – those born between 1981 and 1996[4] – for killing a host of items ranging from napkins and casual dining to the entire Canadian tourism industry and the general concept of loyalty.[5] Drawing on data from a 2014 Reason-Rupert Poll of 2,000 young adults,[6] at least one journalist[7] suggested that political ideology might be another item added to this list of casualties. This survey revealed a number of apparent ideological conflicts. For example, 65 percent of those surveyed thought it would help the economy to cut spending, while at the same time, 62 percent said that it would help the economy to spend more on job training. Similarly, 74 percent thought the government should guarantee that everyone gets enough to eat and a place to sleep, but 66 percent agreed that "when something is run by the government, it is usually inefficient and wasteful." So even though these young adults should be one of the most connected and informed generations in history, the overall picture from these data is that Millennials' political attitudes might best be described as "totally incoherent."

But even the authors of these articles acknowledge that Millennials' opinions may be more organized than the splashy headlines imply. When broken into the

---

[4] Borrowed from the generational cutoffs utilized by the Pew Research Center: www.pewresearch .org/fact-tank/2019/01/17/where-millennials-end-and-generation-z-begins/. Accessed December 28, 2020.

[5] See https://mashable.com/2017/07/31/things-millennials-have-killed/ for a thorough though not exhaustive list. Accessed December 28, 2020.

[6] See https://reason.com/2014/07/10/reason-rupe-2014-millennial-survey/. Accessed December 28, 2020.

[7] www.vox.com/2014/7/14/5891765/millennials-incoherent-politics-libertarians. See also www .theatlantic.com/politics/archive/2014/07/millennials-economics-voting-clueless-kids-these-days/374427/. Both accessed December 28, 2020.

oversimplified dichotomies listed here, it is possible that these views are not completely at odds. Is it really that much of a contradiction to desire the government to spend less in some areas (e.g. defense) but more in others (e.g. welfare)? Moreover, opinions on social issues show more consistency. Almost 70 percent of Millennials surveyed supported same-sex marriage, while 61 percent said that abortion should generally be legal. And finally, we have to keep in mind that all of these figures are at the aggregate level; the beliefs of any one individual Millennial may not be so scattered.

In all, this is just another example of how and why the consistency of individuals' issue preferences needs to be reexamined. While the more incoherent and illogical aspects of people's beliefs may be more likely to make headlines, they often do not tell the full story. Thus, this section offers another look at the organization of individuals' issue opinions. Updating previous works, I use multiple data sets and approaches to explore the connections between opinions on different issues (i.e., what goes with what), the consistency of the same issue positions over time, and how malleable issue positions are when individuals are presented with partisan cues. By the end of the section it should be clear that although Applebees may be dying, stable and relatively consistent issue positions are still very much alive and well among a sizeable portion of the electorate.

2.1 Notes on the Data

This section presents data from multiple sources. To examine the correlations between individuals' issue opinions in a single time period, I use both the 2020 American National Election Studies (ANES) Time Series Study,[8] as well as the six election-year Cooperative Election Study (CES) surveys conducted between 2010 and 2020.[9] Each CES study consists of pre- and postelection online interviews of 50,000+ US adults. To look at the stability of issues over time, I take advantage of the fact that the 2020 ANES reinterviewed (via the internet) 2,839 individuals who completed the 2016 ANES.[10] I also utilize the 2010–2014 CES panel study.[11] The CES panel features 9,500 US adults who were surveyed in 2010, 2012, and again in 2014.

---

[8] Data and documentation available at https://electionstudies.org/data-center/2020-time-series-study/.

[9] Formerly the Cooperative Congressional Election Study. Principle Investigators are Stephen Ansolabehere, Sam Luks, and Brian Schaffner. For more information and all common content CES data utilized here, see https://cces.gov.harvard.edu/.

[10] All data and documentation can be found at https://electionstudies.org/.

[11] Principle Investigators Brian Schaffner and Stephen Ansolabehere. Data and documentation available at https://dataverse.harvard.edu/dataset.xhtml?persistentId=doi%3A10.7910/DVN/TOE8I1.

I provide more detail about the specific questions used in each of the appropriate subsequent subsections.

But before proceeding, it is important to acknowledge that while earlier ANES studies used face-to-face interviews, the majority of the ANES studies I use and all of the CES surveys were conducted online. A number of studies have raised concerns about how differences in both sampling methods and administration mode may hinder comparability. Particularly relevant to my work here are findings that online samples may overrepresent the politically engaged (e.g. Chang and Krosnick 2009) and significantly lower nonresponse (Gooch and Vavreck 2019). Although investigations of both types of surveys used here show few differences across modes (Ansolabehere and Schaffner 2014; Guggenheim et al. 2019), the differences that are found are important. Notably, when comparing the web and face-to-face modes of the 2016 ANES, Guggenheim et al. (2019) find that online respondents had higher levels of political knowledge and significantly different opinions on some of the key issues analyzed here. So while I offer comparisons to previous works to provide context, I do so with the acknowledgment that some of the differences I find may be related not just to a change in the electorate, but also to changes in the way we survey the electorate.

I also take several steps to more directly address issues of comparability. First, when making comparisons, I offer specific notes on how differences in mode may contribute to over- or underestimation of the differences in findings. Second, when looking solely at the 2020 ANES, I present the results for just those interviewed by video or telephone alongside the full sample results. This will provide a fuller picture and enhance my argument, as video samples are most comparable to face-to-face interviews (Endres et al. 2023).

Finally, when analyzing the ANES, I employ a measure of political knowledge that should be more consistent across modes. When working with online surveys, measures that rely on answers to objective political knowledge questions (e.g. "Which party holds the majority in the US House?") can inflate levels of political knowledge because respondents can easily use an internet search to cheat (Smith, Clifford, and Jerit 2020). Prior works, however, show that consistency should not only be related to this type of general political knowledge, but also to more specific knowledge of "what goes with what." That is, parties and elites put issues into liberal and conservative bundles, and when individuals are aware of these positions, they should be more likely to adopt them as their own (Lenz 2012). Specifically, Freeder, Lenz, and Turney (2019) find that the stability of opinions over time increases with greater knowledge of where the parties are placed relative to one another.

Thus, I follow Freeder, Lenz, and Turney (2019) and construct a measure of political knowledge that is derived from where respondents place both the Democratic and Republican presidential candidates on seven-point scales measuring their positions on employment, defense, spending/services, aid to Blacks, and health insurance. For each issue, I consider a respondent correct if they place the Republican, Donald Trump, to the right of (i.e. more conservative than) the Democrat, Joseph Biden. Summing the number of correct relative placements results in a measure that ranges from 0 to 5. This measure is advantageous because while a quick internet search can easily reveal the answer to objective knowledge questions like which party holds the majority in the US House or the party affiliation of one's governor, candidates' positions are typically more difficult to discern. And even if information about the candidates' positions is more readily available, respondents still need to possess the cognitive ability to translate that information to the correct point on the issue scale presented to them.

Table 1 shows the mean levels of knowledge across surveys and modes. To standardize across measures, each is calculated as the mean percentage answered correctly. Only the ANES has the questions needed to construct the placement-based measure of knowledge, but both the CES and the ANES have objective knowledge batteries. Each asks individuals about the party with the majority in the US House and the party with the majority in the US Senate. Beyond that, the CES also asks about the party affiliation of the governor, two US senators, and US House member that represent the respondent. Instead of these more 50/50-type questions, the ANES asks respondents to volunteer the number of years in a full term for a US Senator and to identify which of four programs receives the least funding from the federal government.

When looking at the full objective knowledge batteries, it appears that the CES respondents are more knowledgeable than the ANES respondents. But when only looking at the two common items, this reverses. And though it should be more difficult for respondents to cheat on the placement questions, we see that this measure generally produces the highest estimates of political knowledge. Both of these findings are likely due to the greater difficulty of the two unique objective knowledge items in the ANES battery. Still, there is a fair amount of consistency across modes and, importantly, we see that the online samples do not produce the highest knowledge scores. Whether looking at objective knowledge or relative placements, respondents who took the ANES via video interview – the mode thought to be most akin to face-to-face interviewing (Endres et al. 2023) – scored the highest. So while I take care when presenting results from online studies alongside evidence from earlier, face-to-face surveys, I still see these data as allowing for meaningful comparisons.

Table 1 Comparison of mean knowledge measures, 2020 CES and 2020 ANES

Knowledge measure	2020 CES All online N = 61,000	2020 ANES All modes N = 8,280	2020 ANES Online only N = 7,782	2020 ANES Phone only N = 139	2020 ANES Video only N = 359
% Correct: All objective knowledge questions[a]	0.72	0.55	0.55	0.47	0.57
	(0.34)	(0.30)	(0.30)	(0.26)	(0.30)
% Correct: Common objective knowledge questions	0.67	0.74	0.74	0.71	0.76
	(0.43)	(0.34)	(0.36)	(0.33)	(0.36)
% Correct placements of Trump relative to Biden	Not Available	0.77	0.77	0.70	0.84
		(0.30)	(0.31)	(0.30)	(0.24)

Note: Cell entries are means with standard deviations in parentheses.

[a] The CES and ANES each employ their own set of questions. See Online Appendix for full wording.

2.2 Consistency across Issues

Much of the evidence for a lack of consistency comes from older surveys. For example, Kinder and Kalmoe (2017) use data from 1972–2012. But clearly, the American political landscape has changed quite a bit since then. Thus, I begin with an updated look at the degree to which individuals' opinions in one issue area are related to opinions in another. I begin by looking at the six election-year CES surveys conducted between 2010 and 2020. Though the surveys do not feature the exact same questions, all six feature questions about four major issue areas: guns, immigration, abortion, and the environment.[12]

Table 2 shows the correlations between opinions in these different issue areas. These statistics indicate that there is a fair amount of correspondence between individuals' opinions on these four issues. All but one of the Cronbach's alpha coefficients – which are measures of internal consistency – meet or exceed the 0.70 cutoff that most social science research uses as a standard for reliability, particularly when using a four-item scale (Cortina 1993). Moreover, though the correlation coefficients vary across issues and over time, all averages exceed 0.30 and fall in a range that is typically considered a weak to moderate relationship. The range for the average correlations between pairs is similar, as the highest average correlation is between opinions on guns

Table 2 Correlations between issue opinions, 2010–2020 CES

	2010	2012	2014	2016	2018	2020
Guns and immigration	0.45	0.40	0.38	0.41	0.52	0.44
Guns and abortion	0.31	0.28	0.38	0.40	0.44	0.44
Guns and the environment	0.40	0.33	0.54	0.50	0.58	0.42
Immigration and abortion	0.33	0.28	0.38	0.41	0.58	0.57
Immigration and the environment	0.43	0.36	0.41	0.44	0.61	0.44
Abortion and the environment	0.32	0.31	0.44	0.41	0.56	0.52
Mean correlation across all issue pairs	0.37	0.33	0.42	0.43	0.55	0.47
Chronbach's alpha of issue index	**0.70**	**0.66**	**0.74**	**0.75**	**0.83**	**0.77**

Note: Opinions in each issue area are derived from responses to one or more questions on that topic. See the Appendix for full question wordings.

---

[12] See the Appendix for full question wording.

and the environment ($r = 0.46$), and the lowest average correlation is between opinions on guns and abortion ($r = 0.38$).

But to better put these correlations into context, consider the benchmarks reported in critiques of ideology. When looking at opinions on seven salient issues, Converse (1964) finds an average correlation of 0.11 among his general population sample. The correlation increases to 0.25 when he focuses on an elite sample, but still, both averages are below what I find in the CES. More recently, Kinder and Kalmoe (2017) examine issue opinions from the 1972–2012 ANES surveys and find an average correlation of 0.16. Thus, the CES data suggest a much higher level of constraint than that found by previous studies.

The average correlations between issue areas remain relatively high even when I subset my samples by levels of political knowledge. Using the total number of correct responses to the six questions introduced in section 2.1 as a measure of political knowledge, I find that the CES samples are quite informed; in each survey, at least 33 percent of respondents answered all six questions correctly. So to better assess consistency among the less informed, I calculated the average correlations for those whose responses place them in the bottom 25 percent of that sample year.[13] Figure 1 plots these average correlations and compares them to the averages found when I focus only on those who answered all six questions correctly.

Consistent with what should be expected, Figure 1 shows a clear split based on information; those who answered all six questions correctly have much higher average correlations than those in the bottom 25th percent. If the ability to search for answers and cheat on these objective knowledge questions is driving up the percentage of individuals classified as highly informed, then this is likely an *under*estimate of the constraint among the most informed. And even if there is not cheating but an oversampling of engaged respondents, we still see that the least informed respondents produce averages that hover around the 0.16 benchmark from the 1972–2012 ANES surveys. That is, even the least informed CES respondents display a level of issue consistency that is on par with the consistency observed among earlier samples that also included the most informed. This again suggests that estimates derived from older samples may not accurately capture the level of ideology in today's electorate.

But in addition to possible survey mode concerns, there are other potential issues that must be acknowledged when trying to compare what I find to previous results. First, I have only examined a very small subset of all possible issues.

---

[13] In 2014 and 2016, the lowest 25th percent includes those who answered two or fewer questions correctly. In 2012, 2018, and 2020, this group includes those who answered three or fewer questions correctly. In 2010 – the year with the highest mean level of knowledge – this group includes those who answered four or fewer questions correctly.

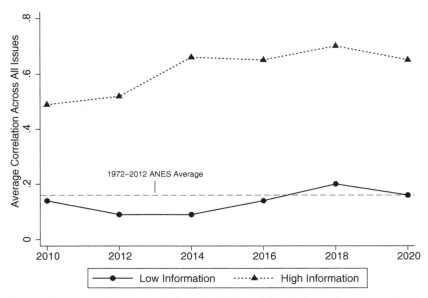

Figure 1 Average issue correlations for high and low information respondents, 2010–2020 CES

Note: See the Appendix for the full wordings of questions used to gauge issue opinions. High information refers to those respondents who answered all six objective knowledge questions correctly. Low information refers to those respondents in the bottom 25 percent of the knowledge scale in that survey year.

The 0.16 benchmark, however, comes from looking at a wider range of issues that includes opinions on things like foreign affairs and defense, which are often believed orthogonal to social and economic preferences (Peffley and Hurwitz 1985). Moreover, whereas most analyses – particularly those that use the ANES – rely on a single question to represent beliefs on an issue, the majority of the issue opinions examined here are indices formed from responses to multiple questions on the topic. While the use of multiple questions reduces bias and yields better estimates of individuals' true, underlying preferences (Ansolabehere, Rodden, and Snyder 2008), it also lends itself to finding higher correlations. Indeed, four of the five lowest correlations presented in Table 1 occur when both issues were measured by a single item.

To offer a more apples-to-apples comparison, then, I turn to the 2020 ANES.[14] Like the 1992 ANES analyzed by Kinder and Kalmoe (2017), the 2020 survey features five questions that use seven-point scales to gauge respondents' opinions on (1) the government's role in providing employment and a good standard of

---

[14] Data and documentation available at https://electionstudies.org/data-center/2020-time-series-study/.

Table 3 Correlations between issue opinions, 2020 ANES

	Employment	Defense	Spending/services	Aid to Blacks
Defense	0.40 (0.21)			
Spending/ services	0.62 (0.39)	0.29 (0.22)		
Aid to Blacks	0.64 (0.56)	0.44 (0.28)	0.55 (0.46)	
Health insurance	0.62 (0.42)	0.48 (0.33)	0.59 (0.53)	0.55 (0.33)

Note: Main entries are correlations from the 2020 ANES. Numbers in parentheses are the 1992 ANES high information correlations reported by Kinder and Kalmoe (2017).

living; (2) levels of defense spending; (3) the amount of services government should provide; (4) government aid to Blacks; and (5) government versus private health insurance.[15] Table 3 shows the correlations between each of these issue areas. For comparison, the corresponding correlations that Kinder and Kalmoe (2017) report for high information respondents are included in parentheses.[16] Comparing the full 2020 ANES sample to just the highly informed from the 1992 ANES, I am offering a stricter test that attempts to account for differences in survey mode.

Table 3 again shows that individuals do appear to have consistent opinions across issues. Even though opinions in each issue area are measured using just one question, the individual correlations and their mean ($r = 0.52$) are comparable to those observed in the CES. In fact, the consistency that I find among the whole sample is actually greater than what Kinder and Kalmoe (2017) observed among just the most informed respondents in the 1992 ANES. This holds even when I restrict my sample to just the video respondents (see the Appendix).[17] Overall, these higher correlations are consistent with Kinder and Kalmoe's (2017) findings of an upward trend over time,[18] though they suggest that the move toward coherence has occurred much faster than originally expected.

---

[15] See the Appendix for full question wordings.   [16] See Table 2.3 on p. 37 of the original text.

[17] There were three instances where the telephone respondents reported lower correlations: aid to Blacks and defense, aid to Blacks and spending/services, and health insurance and spending/services. While further investigation is needed, it should be noted that (1) telephone respondents have a tendency to overselect extreme responses on ordinal scales (Dillman et al. 2009); and (2) the telephone sample had the highest percentage of black respondents – 15.11 percent compared to 10.03 percent of the video sample and 8.60 percent of the internet sample – and this may be impacting opinions on the aid to Blacks question.

[18] See Table 2.1 on p. 29 of the original text.

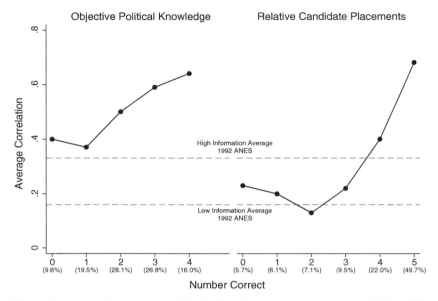

Figure 2 Average issue correlations by number of correct answers, 2020 ANES
Note: Values in parentheses indicate the percentage of respondents falling into that category.

Figure 2 separates respondents out by level of information. I show both measures of knowledge ($r = 0.32$) and plot the high- and low-information means from the 1992 ANES so as to allow for careful comparison. Both measures suggest a relationship between knowledge and the consistency of individuals' own issue opinions, though the two offer slightly different results. Looking first at the objective knowledge measure, we see a greater percentage of respondents at the lower end of the scale, but average correlations that all exceed those found among the most informed in 1992. Turning to the placement measure, we see a greater percentage of respondents at the higher end of the scale, but averages at the lower end that more closely reflect the average observed among the least informed in 1992. But by either measure, the majority of respondents contribute to average correlations that suggest more issue consistency than the most informed quintile of 1992 respondents. All total, then, the correlations presented in this section show clear patterns of organization in the issue opinions of the modern electorate and suggest that reliance on older evidence may lead to the overstatement of ideological innocence.

2.3 Stability over Time

A second way to gauge the amount of ideological thinking in the electorate is to look at the extent to which individuals express the same issue opinion at different points in time. To do this, I draw on two sources of data. The first is the 2010–2014 CES panel study. In all survey years, all respondents were asked a three-question battery about their opinions on immigration,[19] and single questions about their opinions on guns, climate change, abortion, the environment, gay marriage, and affirmative action.[20] I use responses to these questions to examine the stability of responses between 2010 and 2012, 2012 and 2014, and 2010 and 2014.

The second data source is the 2016–2020 ANES panel study. I focus on six issues[21] where respondents placed themselves and both presidential candidates in both survey years – the five ANES issues previously analyzed (employment, defense, spending/services, aid to Blacks, and healthcare) and an additional item that measures opinions on the environment/jobs tradeoff.[22] I use these responses to examine stability between 2016 and 2020.

Figure 3 shows the distributions of the correlations between questions for each possible comparison. Again, I offer a benchmark from Kinder and Kalmoe (2017), who find an average correlation of 0.60 when looking at the stability of issues opinions in five areas for the most informed 20 percent of respondents in the 1992–1996 ANES panel.[23] The stability of opinions on the CES tends to be higher than the stability on the ANES, though they span a slightly wider range. The lowest CES correlations are between people's opinions on a constitutional ban of gay marriage ($r = 0.75$ for 2010–2012, $r = 0.73$ for 2012–2014, and $r = 0.69$ for 2010–2014), while the highest are between people's opinions on the seriousness of the global climate change issue ($r = 0.87$ for 2010–2012, $r = 0.87$ for 2012–2014, and $r = 0.86$ for 2010–2014). The correlations on the ANES are closer together, with an average of 0.60. But even with this observed variation, we see that almost all of these full sample correlations are greater than or on par with what Kinder and Kalmoe (2017) report when looking at just the most informed. So in general, these more recent surveys reveal a good deal more stability in Americans' issue opinions.

---

[19] A fourth question was also asked, but I exclude it from my index since 2010 responses are only available for a subset ($N = 587$) of the sample.

[20] See the Appendix for full question wordings.

[21] In both surveys, respondents were also asked to place themselves and the presidential candidates on the issue of abortion. All self-placements come from the pre-election surveys. But whereas all 2020 presidential candidate placements and the other five 2016 presidential candidate placements were asked on the pre-election survey, the 2016 candidate placements on abortion were asked on the postelection survey. This complicates the use of these placements as an indicator of knowledge used in self-placements and thus, I omit this issue. Moreover, abortion is not included in Kinder and Kalmoe's (2017) examination of stability so omitting this issue allows for a more direct comparison.

[22] See the Appendix for full question wordings.   [23] See p. 39 of the original text.

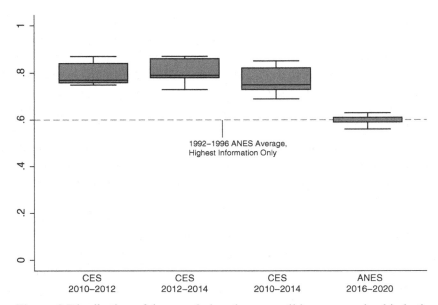

Figure 3 Distribution of the correlations between all issues examined in both survey waves, 2010–2014 CES panel and 2016–2020 ANES panel
Note: See the Appendix for the full wordings of questions used to gauge issue opinions.

As an additional test of attitude stability, I follow prior works (Freeder, Lenz, and Turney 2019; Zaller 1985) and examine the extent to which respondents' attitudes are crystalized. For each issue, an attitude is considered crystalized (coded 1) if the person placed themselves on the same side of the midpoint of the issue scale in both waves and not crystalized (coded 0) if the person placed themselves on different sides of the midpoint, at the midpoint, or "don't know" on either wave. Because this coding scheme requires opinions to be on an ordered scale with a clear midpoint, these analyses are limited to just the 2016–2020 ANES panel.

Based on this classification scheme, the percentage of respondents with crystallized attitudes ranges from 50 percent (on spending/services) to 57 percent (on the environment). This range indicates that on any given issue, a majority of individuals do hold stable opinions. While these are clearly slim majorities ($\overline{X} = 53\%$), they still contradict the idea that only a very limited portion of the population is capable of ideological thinking.

To further reinforce this argument, I show how stability varies with political information. Figure 4 uses the CES panel and plots the mean 2010–2014 correlations by political knowledge, while Figure 5 uses the ANES panel and plots both the mean correlations and mean crystallization scores by the number

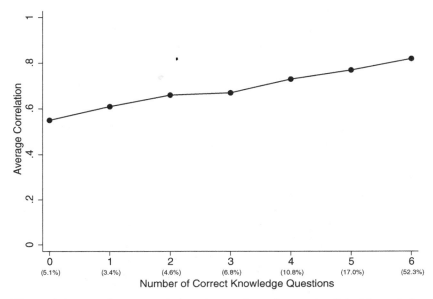

Figure 4 Average issue correlations by number of correct political knowledge responses, 2010–2014 CES panel

Note: Values in parentheses indicate the percentage of respondents falling into that category. An answer is only considered correct if the respondent gave an accurate response in both 2010 and 2014.

of correct presidential candidate placements. For each measure of knowledge, an individual must answer correctly in both survey years in order to be considered correct.

Figure 4 shows that although stability does vary with political knowledge, the gap between the least ($r = 0.55$) and most ($r = 0.82$) informed is not as large as those observed in older data sets. Moreover, only those in the bottom two categories have an average correlation that is below or near the $r = 0.60$ that is observed among the most informed 20 percent in the 1992–1996 ANES panel. That is, over 90 percent of the CES panelists display a level of opinion stability that would generally be considered as consistent with ideological thinking.

Turning to Figure 5, we see that whether looking at the average correlations or the average percentages of respondents with crystallized attitudes, the results are consistent with those reported by Freeder, Lenz, and Turney (2019). By either measure, stability is greatest among those best able to place the parties' candidates on the issues. However, there is one important difference – Figure 5 shows that this more knowledgeable group is larger than it was in 1992–1996. Whereas Freeder, Lenz, and Turney (2019) find that the percentages of respondents who can correctly

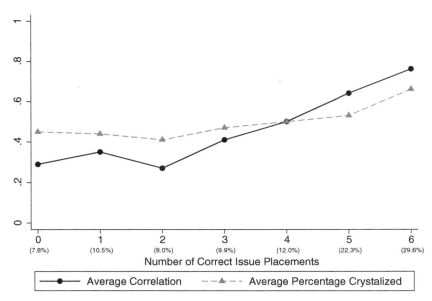

Figure 5 Average issue correlations and crystallization percentages by number of correct placements, 2016–2020 ANES panel
Note: Values in parentheses indicate the percentage of respondents falling into that category. A placement is only considered correct if the respondent gave an accurate response in both 2016 and 2020.

place the candidates on all or all but one of their five featured issues are 19 percent and 18 percent, respectively, I find that in the 2016–2020 panel, these groups comprise 29.6 percent and 22.3 percent of the sample. Since this panel was only conducted online, I cannot speak to how much of this may be due to changes in survey mode. But assuming that at least some of this change is due to actual increases in abilities to know "what goes with what," the end result is an electorate with an increased capacity for holding stable issue opinions.

2.4 Consistency and Stability among Nonidentifiers

In the analyses in the previous section, I account for political knowledge, but do not consider whether or not individuals see themselves as ideological. Although almost all of those who choose "moderate" or "don't know" when initially asked about their ideological identification will choose a label when pressed (see Section 3.1), there are still clear differences between those who more willingly identify as liberal and conservative and those who do not (Kinder and Kalmoe 2017). For example, in the 2020 ANES, nonidentifiers had significantly ($p < 0.00$) lower levels of political knowledge and were

Table 4 Consistency and stability by willingness to identify as ideological, 2020 ANES and 2016–2020 ANES panel

	(1) Average correlation between issues, 2020 ANES	**(2)** Average correlation within issues, 2016–2020 ANES	**(3)** Average percentage of respondents with crystalized opinions, 2016–2020 ANES
Full sample	0.52	0.60	0.53
Ideological identifiers	0.60	0.67	0.58
Moderates	0.27	0.44	0.42
Nonidentifiers	0.30	0.44	0.49

Note: Ideological identification in Column 1 is drawn from the 2020 ANES, while ideological identification for Columns 2 and 3 are drawn from the 2016 ANES.

significantly ($p < 0.00$) less likely to identify with a partisan label or report voting in the 2020 election. Within the full group of nonidentifiers, there were no significant differences in party identification versus pure independence ($p = 0.95$), but moderates were significantly ($p < 0.00$) more knowledgeable and more likely to report voting. Given these differences and the fact that nonidentifiers comprise such large portions of the ANES samples, it is possible that my analyses may be masking a large group of individuals who lack organized ideological thinking.

To address this possibility, I reexamine the consistency and stability of opinions on the ANES.[24] I compute the same averages as previously discussed, but divide the sample into three groups: those who initially identify with one of the six ideological labels (63.3% of the 2020 sample; 59.8% of the 2016–2020 panel), those who identify as moderate (22.0% of the 2020 sample; 20.6% of the 2016–2020 panel), and those who offer no response (14.8% of the 2020 sample; 19.6% of the 2016–2020 panel). These results are displayed in Table 4, which also includes the full sample means for ease of comparison.

The results in Table 4 are in line with what should be expected. The averages calculated when excluding nonidentifiers are greater than the full sample estimates, while the averages focusing solely on moderates and nonidentifiers are smaller than the full sample averages. But even though these figures suggest lower levels of opinion consistency and stability among those who opt to avoid

---

[24] I focus only on the ANES, as the CES has very few nonresponders. See Section 3.1 for more detail on the prevalence of placement.

an ideological label, they are still above what should be considered completely devoid of ideology. The average correlations between 2020 issue opinions are above the 1972–2012 ANES full sample average (0.16), and the stability averages are on par with those obtained when looking at those around the middle of the political information scale (see Figure 5). So while the opinions of individuals who avoid ideological labels may be less coherent than the opinions of those who do opt to use ideological labels, the evidence presented here suggests that writing them off as completely nonideological would be a mischaracterization.

2.5 The (Im)moveability of Preferences

In addition to the type of correlations already presented, critics of ideology also point to experiments that show individuals will shift their issue opinions in response to partisan cues as evidence of a lack of ideological thinking. Upon closer examination, however, the evidence of this type of opinion movement is quite limited. First, generic cues that just signal the position of the party in general or a partisan group (e.g. Republicans in Congress) tend to have no significant effects (Barber and Pope 2019; Nicholson 2012). Rather, it seems people are most responsive to positions when they are attributed to specific party leaders. But even then, different experimental setups produce different patterns of results. For example, Nicholson (2012) finds that treatments cueing Barack Obama, John McCain, and George W. Bush significantly affect the opinions of outpartisans but not inpartisans, while Barber and Pope's (2019) use of treatments featuring Donald Trump and Obama instead yield predominantly inpartisan affects. Moreover, Barber and Pope's (2019) inparty effects are limited to just a subset of the ten issues tested,[25] and are concentrated among the least knowledgeable and most loyal Republicans. In sum, it seems that party leaders' abilities to move issue opinions are far from universal.

As a further test, I conducted an experiment akin to that run by Barber and Pope (2019). The experiment was embedded in an original survey of US adults ($N = 2,205$) administered via the Lucid Fulcrum Exchange platform in September of 2019.[26] The experimental setup was simple. All respondents were asked to indicate whether they supported or opposed a particular

---

[25] Results in Barber and Pope's (2019) Supplementary Materials (Figure A5) show that the liberal Trump treatments affect opinions on six issues (school guns, tax increases, minimum wage, Iran agreement, climate change, and immigration), while conservative Trump treatments only affect opinions on two of the ten issues (guns background and abortion).

[26] See the Appendix for sample demographics. For more on the validation of experimental results obtained via Lucid, see Coppock and McClellan (2019).

Table 5 Overview of the party leader experimental treatments, 2019 Lucid sample

Policy wording	Treatment wording
Keeping the agreement with Iran to limit their obtaining nuclear weapons.	For: Donald Trump has said that he supports the current agreement and would enforce the deal Against: Donald Trump has said that he opposes the current agreement and would renegotiate the deal. Control: No cue
Acknowledging that humans are the largest contributing factor in global climate change.	For: Donald Trump has said that he believes this to be true. Against: Donald Trump has said that he does not believe this to be true. Control: No cue
Extending the number of circumstances where federal funds can be used to pay for abortion.	For: Joseph Biden has expressed support for extending current provisions. Against: Joseph Biden has expressed opposition to extending current provisions. Control: No cue
Increasing regulations on trade with China.	For: Joseph Biden has expressed worry about China and indicated that he perceives a real threat. Against: Joseph Biden has downplayed the need to address China and indicated that he does not perceive a real threat. Control: No cue

policy.[27] If the person was randomly assigned to the control group, there was no additional information. If the person was randomly assigned to one of the two treatment groups, then they were told that a prominent party leader was either for or against the policy. This was repeated four times so that each respondent gave opinions on four different issues. Table 5 gives an overview of the issues and party leaders used.

---

[27] Half of respondents also had a "Don't Know" option. Following Barber and Pope (2019), I focus only on those who select favor or oppose. Both groups of respondents are analyzed together, with a control for which of the two sets of response options was presented.

The four issues were shown in random order. Each issue was selected because the specific leader – either Trump or Biden – has actually taken both sides of the issue and thus, respondents should see either the for or against treatment as plausible. The two Trump issues were selected from the ten used by Barber and Pope (2019). Since these were the only two issues where Trump's position cues significantly moved both Republican and Democratic respondents in those original experiments, my use of these two issues makes this is a more than fair and comparable test of the malleability of individuals' opinions.

Given that past works indicate that reactions to party leader cues vary across individuals, I analyze how the treatment effects differ based on both political knowledge[28] and strength of party identification. Tables 6 and 7 summarize the results for the two Trump issues.[29] These tables show very few statistically significant effects. While most Republicans adopted Trump's position on Iran, the treatments had more minimal effects on their opinions on climate change. When looking at Democratic respondents, the most knowledgeable were more likely to oppose the Iran agreement when told Trump supported it, but those Democrats told that Trump was against the Iran agreement and those in either of the climate treatment groups did not shift their opinions.

I do not include similar tables for the Biden treatments because none of the treatments yield significant effects. Full results are available in the Appendix, but whether looking at abortion or trade with China, neither Republicans nor Democrats shifted opinions in response to being told Biden's position. It could be that Biden was not viewed as the party leader at the time the survey was administered; although he was the former vice president and a leading Democratic presidential candidate, he was not yet the party's official nominee. Thus, it is possible that Biden's positions did not carry the same persuasive weight or polarizing power as Trump's.

To address this possibility, I recruited 1,200 US adults via Amazon's Mechanical Turk (MTurk) and reran the Biden portion of the experiment in July 2021.[30] Table 8 shows the results by partisan extremity. While I do find treatment effects in this iteration of the experiment, the Biden cue is still only

---

[28] Political knowledge was measured by four multiple choice questions: (1) who has the last say when there is conflict over the meaning of the Constitution? (the Supreme Court, the president, Congress); (2) who is the Chief Justice of the U.S. Supreme Court? (John Roberts, Mike Pence, Clarence Thomas, Paul Ryan); (3) who is the current U.S. Senate majority leader? (Nancy Pelosi, Kevin McCarthy, Mitch McConnell, Chuck Shumer); and (4) how much of a majority is needed to overturn a presidential veto? (one-half, two-thirds, three-fifths, three-fourths).

[29] Full model results are available in the Appendix.

[30] The experiment was embedded within a larger study. Although a convenience sample, previous research supports the validity and generalizability of results obtained from the MTurk platform (Clifford, Jewell, and Waggoner 2015; Krupnikov and Levine 2014). See the Appendix for more information on the sample demographics.

Table 6 Effects of Trump cues on issue opinions, Democratic respondents, 2019 Lucid sample

	Iran		Climate change	
	Trump for vs. Control	Trump against vs. Control	Trump for vs. Control	Trump against vs. Control
By knowledge				
0 Correct	No difference	No difference	No difference	No difference
1 Correct	No difference	No difference	No difference	No difference
2 Correct	−0.11	No difference	No difference	No difference
3 Correct	−0.12	No difference	No difference	No difference
4 Correct	−0.13	No difference	No difference	No difference
By partisan strength				
Leaner	−0.20	No difference	No difference	No difference
Weak	No difference	No difference	No difference	No difference
Strong	−0.10	No difference	No difference	No difference

Note: Numeric entries are changes in the probability of selecting "for" vs. "against" when asked about keeping the Iran agreement or acknowledging the human role in climate change when comparing the treatment to the control ($p < 0.05$). "No difference" indicates that the effect of the treatment was not statistically significant ($p < 0.05$). Full results are available in the Appendix. $N = 903$ for each issue.

Table 7 Effects of Trump cues on issue opinions, Republican respondents, 2019 Lucid sample

	Iran		Climate change	
	Trump for vs. Control	Trump against vs. Control	Trump for vs. Control	Trump against vs. Control
By knowledge				
0 Correct	No difference	No difference	No difference	No difference
1 Correct	No difference	No difference	No difference	No difference
2 Correct	0.13	−0.20	No difference	No difference
3 Correct	0.18	−0.25	0.10	No difference
4 Correct	0.22	−0.27	0.16	No difference
By partisan strength				
Leaner	No difference	−0.34	No difference	No difference
Weak	0.16	No difference	No difference	No difference
Strong	0.20	−0.16	0.15	No difference

Note: Numeric entries are changes in the probability of selecting "for" vs. "against" when asked about keeping the Iran agreement or acknowledging the human role in climate change when comparing the treatment to the control ($p < 0.05$). "No difference" indicates that the effect of the treatment was not statistically significant ($p < 0.05$). Full results are available in the Appendix. $N = 650$ for Iran and 657 for climate.

Table 8 Effects of Biden cues on issue opinions, 2021 MTurk sample

	Abortion		China	
	Biden for vs. Control	Biden against vs. Control	Biden for vs. Control	Biden against vs. Control
Democrats				
Leaner	No difference	No difference	No difference	No difference
Weak	0.27	0.26	0.27	No difference
Strong	No difference	No difference	No difference	No difference
Republicans				
Leaner	No difference	No difference	0.28	No difference
Weak	No difference	No difference	No difference	No difference
Strong	No difference	No difference	No difference	No difference

Note: Numeric entries are changes in the probability of selecting "for" vs. "against" when asked about expanding federal funding for abortion or increasing Chinese trade regulations when comparing the treatment to the control ($p < 0.05$). "No difference" indicates that the effect of the treatment was not statistically significant ($p < 0.05$). Full results are available in the Appendix. $N = 703$ and $N = 704$ for Democrats; $N = 430$ and $N = 432$ for Republicans.

significant in four of the twenty-four possible instances. And in two of those instances, my findings are counter to expectations; weak Democrats move in the opposite direction of Biden on abortion and weak Republicans move in the same direction as Biden on trade with China. I cannot test for the effects of political knowledge, as this MTurk study did not include any questions that would allow me to construct an appropriate measure. But still, my inability to consistently find significant results for both leaders or on all issues further suggests that individuals' opinions can only be moved under limited circumstances.

The lack of significant effects is especially striking given that the party cue was the *only* additional piece of information that individuals in the treatment groups were given. A growing number of works (Boudreau and Mackenzie 2014; Bullock 2011; Mullinix 2016; Ozer 2020) show that the effects of party cues become even more muted when presented in conjunction with other policy-relevant information. For example, Chong and Mullinix's (2019) experimental work finds that policy information can have effects that rival or even exceed those of party, leading them to conclude that "people can take and maintain positions on issues despite shifting party cues" (p. 1230). So while there certainly are instances where individuals prioritize party above all else, these seem to be more of an exception than a rule.

2.6 In Summation

When people critique Americans for a lack of meaningful issue positions, they often point to three key pieces evidence: (1) the consistency between opinions on different issues; (2) the stability of opinions over time; (3) the extent to which opinions can be changed by party cues. In this section, I have reexamined all three and the results that I find show an electorate whose opinions are far from incoherent. Using multiple surveys that ask about different issues and rely on different question formats, I find a considerable degree of consistency and stability. In addition, my experimental work reiterates that movement in response to party leaders' positions is limited.

Of course, it needs to be acknowledged that the issues explored in this section all tended to be highly salient and politicized issues; the fact that many individuals were unable to form consistent opinions across these "easy" issues suggests that regardless of changes to the political environment, there will always be those who should be classified as ideologically innocent. But still, my findings show improvement in constraint across salient issues, and, coupled with evidence that individuals can process less salient issues in a logical manner (Dias and Lelkes 2022), suggest that a nontrivial portion of the electorate does appear to know "what goes with what" and consistently express opinions seemingly correlated with that knowledge. Even those who avoid ideological labels or who have limited political knowledge still display a level of constraint. It then becomes a question of whether individuals draw on these issue opinions when thinking about ideological labels. Are these labels just symbolic identifications? This is a matter that will be explored in the next section.

3 The Use and Meaning of Ideological Labels

When only asked a single question about partisanship or ideology, a large portion of Americans avoid labeling their political beliefs. Repeated public opinion polling shows that between 2011 and 2021, anywhere from 35 percent to 50 percent of respondents said they were independent,[31] while the proportion of respondents identifying as moderate consistently hovered around 36 percent.[32] But as research on independents shows (Keith et al. 1992; Klar and Krupnikov 2016), these initial responses do not tell the full story; many people who initially identify as independents actually think and behave in a distinctively partisan manner. Further probing of individuals who claim to be moderate, however, is lacking.[33]

Thus in this section, I take another look at unwillingness to select an ideological label. In addition, I use open-ended responses to better understand just what individuals mean when they identify as liberal, conservative, or moderate. Finally, I show that a more explicit version of the ideological placement question can improve the relationship between identification and underlying issue preferences. Together, these last two subsections suggest that policy preferences play a prominent role in determining how people identify themselves. And altogether, my findings suggest that to truly assess the prevalence of ideological thinking in the electorate, we must start by asking the right questions.

3.1 Undercounting Ideologues

As noted in Section 1, one of the major critiques of ideology is rooted in the fact that a majority of 1972–2012 ANES respondents do not choose an ideological identification. I contend that relying on these older numbers may be misleading for at least three major reasons. First, while the ANES is a well-regarded, scientific survey, it is just one source. The CES, which also employs transparent scientific methodology, yields a substantially lower nonresponse rate. In the 2010–2020 election-year studies, the percentage of CES respondents

---

[31] https://news.gallup.com/poll/15370/party-affiliation.aspx. Accessed January 20, 2022.

[32] https://news.gallup.com/poll/388988/political-ideology-steady-conservatives-moderates-tie.aspx. Accessed January 20, 2022.

[33] For a notable and promising exception, see Fowler et al. (2022).

choosing "don't know" ranges from 3.06 to 6.46. And importantly, this does not translate into a larger percentage of individuals choosing "moderate." Similar to what is observed in the ANES, the percentage of CES respondents choosing "moderate" ranges from 19.30 to 26.05. Thus, the CES presents an electorate where almost two-thirds of individuals consider themselves to be ideological.

There are, of course, a number of differences in the modes and samples of the two types of surveys (see Ansolabehere and Rivers 2013). But some of the differences in ideological responses may also be due to the recency of the data. A closer look at the ANES reveals that use of the "don't know" or "haven't thought much about this" options declines quite a bit over time. Indeed, Table 9 presents a comparison of the responses reported by Kinder and Kalmoe (2017, p. 54) and the responses given to the most recent ANES surveys.

In the more recent studies, the percentage of "don't know" responses drops considerably and this is no longer the most prevalent category – even if I omit those who completed their interview online. The "moderate" category is still relatively large, but the overall percentage of ideologues exceeds 60 percent and is much more in line with the CES.

Finally, even if individuals decline to choose an ideological label when asked a single question, further probing may reveal a liberal or conservative leaning. This is not a new idea; in both 1989 and 2000, the ANES experimented with branching-type ideological questions that first asked for identification and then

Table 9 Distribution of ideological identification, older versus newer ANES

Identification	1972–2012 ANES	2016 and 2020 ANES full	2016 and 2020 ANES omitting online
Extremely liberal	1.8%	4.0%	4.1%
Liberal	7.8%	14.2%	13.4%
Slightly liberal	9.1%	11.2%	10.7%
Moderate; middle of the road	24.5%	22.4%	21.6%
Slightly conservative	13.6%	10.6%	12.9%
Conservative	13.3%	18.0%	16.5%
Extremely conservative	2.4%	4.6%	3.3%
Don't know/haven't thought much about this	27.5%	15.1%	17.5%

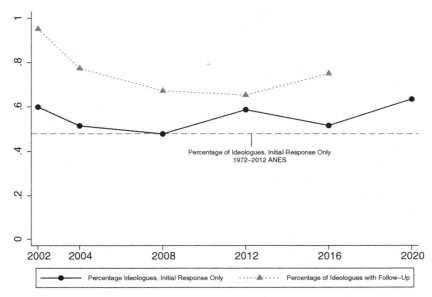

Figure 6 Percentage of ideologues with and without the follow-up question, 2002–2020 ANES

asked about the strength of that attachment. Though branching can help push people away from defaulting to the middle option (Aldrich et al. 1982), this experiment yielded little evidence of improvement over the standard format (Kinder and Kalmoe 2017; Krosnick and Berent 1993; Malhotra, Krosnick, and Thomas 2009; Treier and Hillygus 2009).

Still, the ANES has followed up with those who select "moderate" or "don't know" since 2002.[34] These individuals are asked "If you had to choose, would you consider yourself a liberal or conservative?" Though this suggests a forced choice, respondents could still select moderate, don't know, or refuse to choose. Figure 6 plots the total percentage of respondents who give an ideological response (1) to the first question (solid line); and (2) once I include those who choose liberal or conservative when pressed (dotted line). I do not plot the follow-up results for 2020, since "moderate" was omitted from the choice set in these interviews. For reference, I also plot the 48 percent that Kinder and Kalmoe (2017) report as the total who are ideological on the 1972–2012 ANES surveys.

The solid line in Figure 6 again illustrates the importance of considering more recent data. In all but 2008, ideological identifiers are actually the majority. Even

---

[34] The follow-ups began in 1984, but in 1984, 1986, 1990, and 1994 only those who answered "don't know" received second question. The data from 2000 are not comparable since it includes a subset of respondents who received the experimental branching format.

when only asked the single, standard question, an average of 55.5 percent of respondents choose some type of liberal or conservative label. Moreover, these percentages all increase once I include the follow-up question. In almost all cases, the majority of individuals who initially selected "moderate" or "don't know" will choose "liberal" or "conservative" when pressed. And even if I restrict my samples to just those who were interviewed face-to-face, the percentage of overall ideologues increases from 46.7 to 69.7 in 2012 and from 75.1 to 86.0 in 2016. Thus, it appears that failing to consider responses to this simple follow-up leads to an underestimation of proportion of ideologues in the electorate.

Of course, there is likely a subset of individuals who truly have no ideological identity but who choose a label simply to advance to the next question on the survey. And, as work on independents shows us (e.g. Klar and Krupnikov 2016), there are also likely important differences between those who initially choose an ideological label and those who only do so when given a follow-up. Even so, the data in Table 4 suggest that a good number who pick a label when pressed do think in a somewhat ideological fashion. The correlations between the issue opinions of reluctant identifiers are weaker than those observed among those who initially identify as ideological, but they are still stronger than would be expected if these individuals were truly devoid of ideology. There is still a great deal more work to be done on understanding nonidentifiers, but the data presented in this section all make the case that the group in need of study is generally smaller than typically assumed

3.2 Not Just What, but Why

Although I have shown that a majority of people do think of themselves as either liberal or conservative, this does not necessarily mean that their choices are reflective of their underlying issue opinions. The terms "liberal" and "conservative" are somewhat abstract and open to the interpretation of the survey respondent. Some individuals may choose labels that they see as corresponding with their preferences, while others may select labels based on social groups, identities, or affect (e.g. Ellis and Stimson 2012; Mason 2018), and still others may be choosing almost at random. Over the years, political scientists have used a number of different techniques to better standardize measures of ideology (Aldrich and Mckelvey 1977; Hare et al. 2015; Simas 2018; Wand 2013). Here, I take a somewhat straightforward approach: I look at what people say when they are asked about what they mean when they use ideological labels. Across three different data sets, I find that the most common understandings do include references to issues, suggesting that much of the electorate is capable of thinking ideologically.

3.2.1 Describing Others as Liberal or Conservative

The 1992 ANES postelection interview including the following open-ended questions:[35]

> People have different things in mind when they say that someone's political views are liberal or conservative. We'd like to know more about this. Let's start with liberal. What sorts of things do you have in mind when you say someone's political views are liberal?
>
> And what do you have in mind when you say that someone's political views are conservative?

In both cases, interviewers were prompted to probe and follow up with "anything else?" until the respondent said "No." Up to three responses for each respondent are coded in the publicly available dataset.

In total, 72.16 percent of respondents offered at a response for at least one ideological term. The result is over 2,700 unique responses for each term, which can be sorted into six broad categories.[36] The frequencies of each type are displayed in Figure 7. Despite some arguments that ideology is mostly symbolic, the least common categories are those that reflect a more identity-based conception of ideology – "Groups," which includes statements referencing those particularly helped or harmed by either liberals or conservatives and "Party," which includes statements referencing the Democratic or Republican parties and/or their members.

Instead, the vast majority of statements reference policy either specifically or in the abstract. The most common responses are those classified as "General Philosophy." Over half of all responses about each of the ideological labels fall into this category. Statements falling into this category pertain to such things as acceptance of/resistance to change and more general references to social welfare, free enterprise, and government.

More specific policy mentions are less common, but still prevalent. These comments are separated into three additional categories. The "Economic Policy" category includes those statements that reference fiscal policy or spending. For example, the most common type of liberal response mentions favoring government spending, while the most common type of conservative response mentions opposing government spending. The "Domestic Policy" category is

---

[35] Variables V926109-V926114. See also the appendix to the 1992 ANES codebook.

[36] The original ANES coding includes seven substantive categories, as the Domestic Policy category is split into those comments referencing a policy that is favored by liberals/conservatives and those referencing a policy that is opposed by liberals/conservatives. For ease of presentation, I combine these. In addition, whereas the ANES coding includes party mentions in the category "other miscellaneous," I treat it as its own category. The remaining "other miscellaneous" responses comprise less than 1 percent of all responses about each ideological label so as such, I omit them from the graphical presentation.

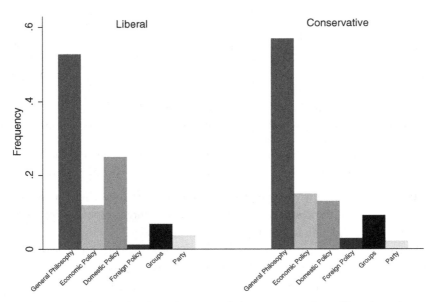

Figure 7 Categorization of open-ended statements about liberals and
conservatives, 1992 ANES

largely dominated by mentions of abortion (25.29 percent of liberal domestic
policy mentions, 41.13 percent of conservative domestic policy mentions), but
also contains statements about a wide range of policies from social security to
civil rights. The "Foreign Policy" category is the smallest of the three policy
categories, and mostly contains references to national security.

Further examination of these data reveals that the tendency toward policy-
based statements is not exclusive to those who consider themselves ideologues.
Table 10 shows that although those who chose "moderate" or "don't know/
haven't though much about this" were less likely to offer at least one open-
ended response, (1) more than half of them did; and (2) the responses that were
given follow the same general pattern of those provided by the more ideological
respondents. This again suggests important heterogeneity in a group that is
often blanketly dismissed as nonideological and shows a widespread ability to
connect ideological labels to policy, regardless of whether one chooses an
ideological label for themself.

3.2.2 Describing Yourself as Liberal or Conservative

Though the open-ended responses from the 1992 ANES are informative, the
questions prompt individuals to think about what comes to mind when they
describe others. It is certainly possible that individuals have different reasons

Table 10 Open-ended statements offered by identifiers and nonidentifiers, 1992 ANES

	Ideological identifiers $N = 1,032$	Nonidentifiers $N = 1,028$
Respondents offering at least one answer	86.82%	57.78%
Total number of responses	3,596	1,879
Responses by category:		
General Philosophy	54.06%	56.25%
Economic Policy	12.12%	15.97%
Domestic Policy	20.72%	15.65%
Foreign Policy	2.28%	1.60%
Groups	8.26%	7.34%
Party	2.09%	2.39%

Note: Percentages may not add to 100 due to rounding and the omission of the small "Other" category.

for choosing the way they describe themselves. In addition, much of my argument is predicated on the idea that more current data is needed to accurately describe the modern electorate. So with this in mind, I placed an open-ended question on an original 1,000-person module of the 2018 CES.

On the postelection wave of the survey, respondents were reminded of the ideological label (very liberal, liberal, somewhat liberal, somewhat conservative, conservative, or very conservative) that they chose during the pre-election wave. Then they were asked to give a brief explanation of why they chose that response. Of the 625 ideologues who completed the postelection survey, only 54 (8.64 percent) did not provide a valid answer[37] and only 6 (<1 percent) said "don't know." I coded the remaining responses in a manner similar to that used by the ANES. I also added a seventh category that I label as "Identity." Responses like "I am a conservative Republican always have been and always will be!" and "because I am" are placed in this category because they signal how respondents see themselves, not their beliefs. And unlike the ANES, the "Other" category is sizeable enough to be included in the presentation. This category contains responses like "I don't really voice my opinions about politics" or "It's the right thing to do."

Figure 8 shows the frequencies of the different categories of responses. Note that although the majority of responses (64.96 percent) fit into just one category,

---

[37] I treat those who replied "n/a," who just repeated or refuted their previously chosen ideological label, or who gave any other type of nonsubstantive response as missing.

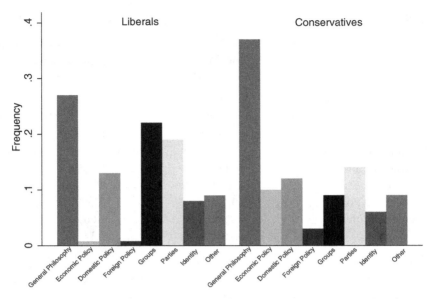

Figure 8 Categorization of open-ended statements about liberal and
conservative self-identification, 2018 CES

some responses are coded as falling into more than one category. For example,
the statement "I chose this as it best represents my beliefs, such as Universal
Health Care, equal pay, protecting the environment, protecting the LGBTQ
Community" is coded as both "Domestic Policy" and "Groups."

When compared to the more general descriptions given on the 1992 ANES,
respondents – and in particular, liberal respondents – are more likely to refer to
groups or parties. Indeed, the wording of many of the open-ended responses
suggests that a good number of respondents view and use partisan and ideological terms interchangeably. But even with the increase in mentions of groups
and parties, the four more issue-based categories are still quite prevalent. Of
those giving valid responses, 70.66 percent of liberals and 73.53 percent of
conservatives gave justifications that are coded in at least one of these categories. Thus, it seems that the majority of people do connect their ideological
identifications to either general or specific policy beliefs.

3.2.3 The Meaning of "Moderate"

To this point, I have ignored the large portion of Americans who identify as
"moderate" or "middle of the road." In their discussion of individuals who
gravitate toward this option, Kinder and Kalmoe (2017) find little difference
between moderates and those who decline to answer, ultimately concluding that

"the 'moderate' category seems less an ideological destination than a refuge for the innocent or confused" (p. 70).

To better assess this statement, I included an open-ended question on the 2019 Lucid survey also analyzed in Section 2.4. This question asked all individuals who selected the midpoint of the ideological scale to give a brief explanation of why they chose that option. Of the 747 respondents (34.25 percent of the sample) who described themselves as "moderate; middle of the road," 93.44 percent gave usable answers to this follow-up.[38] The answers were quite diverse, but I code each as falling into one of eight broad categories.

As might be expected, there are many individuals whose answers indicate that they do not understand the use or meaning of ideological labels and many who state they have no interest in politics. I group all of these respondents into the category "Don't Know/Don't Care."

However, the majority of respondents do offer more meaningful responses. First, similar to the close-ended follow-up, the open-ended follow-up revealed a number of moderates who actually do consider themselves ideological. This category, which is refer to as "Actual Identifier" includes respondents who made statements such as "I'm not a liberal but I lean that way" and "I believe I am in the middle of most political topics, I could lean a little conservative when it comes to finance and social issues."

Next, there are those who might also be considered ideological in that they seem to fit the more traditional, ideological definition of a moderate – those who have both liberal and conservative policy views. I refer to this category as "Both Sides" and include any responses that suggest the individual is a combination of/between the two ends of the ideological spectrum. Though these responses vary in their use of general versus specific or ideological versus partisan terms (e.g. "I'm a social liberal and economic conservative" vs. "Because I agree with both sides on some things"), I include all that indicate the respondent feels at least some association with both the right and the left.

Given evidence that positive and negative political identities are distinct and should be treated as such (e.g. Bankert 2021), I create a third category for those who expressed that they were *not* associated with either side. Examples of statements that are coded into this category include "Because I am not a liberal or a conservative" and "Because the left and right are both crazy and they are getting worse."

Related but somewhat different are those who say they choose "moderate" because they want to remain neutral and/or open-minded or because they do not want to pick sides. This category, which I refer to as "Neutral/Open-Minded,"

---

[38] About half of this group left the box blank, while the other half did things like simply repeating the word "moderate," typing strings of random letters or words, or saying "n/a."

includes statements like "Don't want to pick between the groups" and "I don't have a preference and I am very open minded." I treat this as distinct from the "Both Sides" and "Neither Side" categories because these statements are less about what the person is or is not and more about how the person wants to portray themself.

The appearance of fairness or neutrality may also be at play in the category "Depends on Candidates/Leaders." I use this label to refer the group of respondents who say things like "Because I tend to vote for the person I feel is best qualified no matter the party" and "I vote according to who has the better political history and I feel can/will back up their promises no matter what party they come from." A key distinction between this category and the "Neutral/Open-Minded" is the emphasis on people rather than the groups.

The last more substantive category that I define is "Not Extreme." Responses like "Because I don't think I'm an extreme of anything" and "The only thing I'm 'fanatic' about is my hatred of fanatics" are coded into this category because they indicate an avoidance of the most ardent political views. I treat this as distinct from "Both Sides" because individuals in this category may in fact be one side of the spectrum, but just not in an extreme way.

Finally, I group the remaining responses into the broad category of "Other." Statements coded as "Other" run the gamut from things like "Because I only believe in things that make sense" and "Just want peace" to "I am a proud third generation New Yorker; each to his or her own."

Table 11 shows how respondents are distributed across these categories. Though those who may clearly be called "innocent or confused" make up about 17 percent of moderate respondents, more than twice as many are in the two categories – "Both Sides" and "Actual Identifier" – that are more clearly linked to ideological thinking. My assertion that individuals in these two categories should not necessarily be dismissed as nonideological is supported by the second column in Table 7, which shows each group's mean score on the four-question political knowledge battery that was included in the survey.[39] Given that political knowledge and information are such key predictors of ideological thinking, it is quite telling that individuals in these two categories have significantly higher levels of political knowledge than those in the "Don't Know/Don't Care" category. In fact, the group means for the "Both Sides" and "Actual Identifier" categories are also both significantly ($p < 0.05$) higher than the means for all those who initially identify with an ideological label ($\overline{X} = 1.83$, s.d. = 1.50). The last column also shows that percentage of party identifiers in each of these two categories is higher than the percentage of partisan identifiers who also choose an ideological label (71.80 percent), though the difference is

---

[39] See footnote 25.

Table 11 Categorization of open-ended statements about moderate
self-identification and political knowledge, 2019 Lucid sample

Category	Percentage of respondents	Mean political knowledge score	Percentage of partisan identifiers
Both Sides	35.67%	2.38 (1.23)[a,b]	72.69%[a]
Neither Side	14.18%	2.05 (1.36)[a]	52.53%[b]
Neutral/ Open-Minded	4.87%	1.71 (1.19)	55.88%
Depends on Candidates/ Leaders	3.58%	2.08 (1.04)[a]	84.21%[a]
Actual Identifier	2.87%	2.40 (1.10)[a,b]	95.00%[a,b]
Not Extreme	2.72%	2.63 (1.21)[a,b]	48.00%
Other	18.91%	2.07 (1.26)[a]	73.48%[a]
Don't Know/Don't Care	17.19%	1.58 (1.16)	54.17%[b]

Note: Standard deviations of the mean political knowledge scores are shown in parentheses.
[a] Different from Don't Know/Don't Care at $p < 0.05$.
[b] Different from all ideological identifiers in the full sample at $p < 0.05$.

only statistically significant for the "Actual Identifier" category. Thus, this is suggestive that at least one sizeable subset of moderates should be considered as capable of ideological thinking.[40]

The remaining categories, their corresponding political knowledge scores, and their tendencies toward partisan identification also highlight the heterogeneity of the group known as moderates. Overall, it appears that my work reinforces Ellis and Stimson's (2012) argument that the blanket assumption that those who pick "moderate; middle of the road" lack the willingness or ability to think ideologically needs to be reconsidered. Clearly, individuals have many reasons for choosing to place themselves at the middle, and some of them do appear to be linked to their underlying beliefs.

3.3 Clarifying the Question

Though the open-ended responses presented in the previous section suggest that a majority of individuals view ideological labels as representations of their issue

---

[40] This is also consistent with Fowler et al. (2022), who find evidence of coherent ideology among self-identified moderates.

positions, there is still a sizeable portion of respondents who do not make that connection. While it could be, as critics of ideology contend, that these individuals are simply not capable of this kind of ideological thinking, it may also be that the traditional ideological question is not specific or direct enough. As discussed in Section 1, ideology has both operational and symbolic components. Standard formats of the ideological question, however, do not clearly signal which component respondents should draw on when choosing their own placement.

Since 1972, the ANES has introduced the ideological placement question by telling respondents "We hear a lot of talk these days about liberals and conservatives. Here is a seven-point scale on which the political views that people might hold are arranged from extremely liberal to extremely conservative." While this does note that the scale represents political views, the specific mention of liberals and conservatives also introduces a reminder that these are identities. And after this introduction, respondents are asked to place themselves – not their issue positions – on the scale. This again creates the possibility that respondents are regarding the points on the scale as identifications and not just descriptors of their underlying predispositions.

The format currently used by the CES is also vague. Since 2012, ideological self-placement has been included in a grid that is simply introduced by asking "How would you rate each of the following individuals and groups?" Respondents are again asked to rate themselves, not their issue positions, and just what exactly respondents are rating is ambiguous. Moreover, symbolic ideological concerns may be triggered by the fact that distinctly political and polarizing figures such as presidential candidates are included in this grid, as respondents' affect toward these figures may lead them alter their self-placements relative to where they place the others. For example, an individual may recognize their political views as conservative, but because they dislike Donald Trump, whom they label as conservative, they may alter their self-placement and choose a more moderate or even liberal point on the scale.

With this in mind, I tested a unique, operational version of an ideological placement question on my 1,000-person 2018 CES module. Figure 9 contains a screen shot of the question as it was displayed to respondents. The question targets operational ideology by focusing on policies rather than identity, and uses numerical responses so that respondents can avoid having to select labels that might prime more symbolic concerns. Note that the order in which conservative and liberal were presented was randomized and that the two responses had to sum to 100.

I expect that by not requiring respondents to choose an ideological label, this question format should increase the correlation between identification and policy

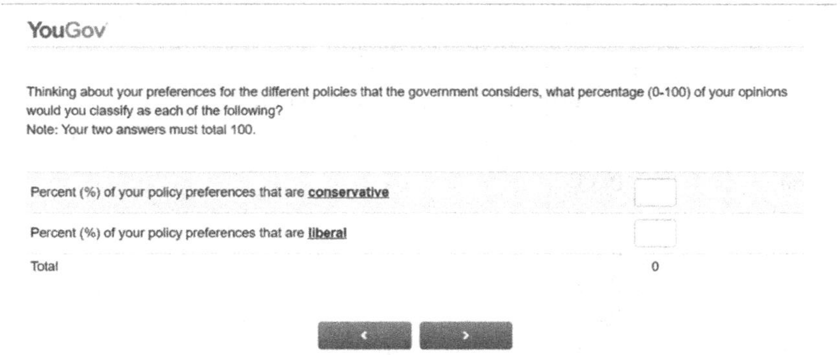

YouGov

Thinking about your preferences for the different policies that the government considers, what percentage (0-100) of your opinions would you classify as each of the following?
Note: Your two answers must total 100.

Percent (%) of your policy preferences that are **conservative**

Percent (%) of your policy preferences that are **liberal**

Total   0

Figure 9 Screenshot of the operational ideology placement question, 2018 CES

preferences. To test this, I compare (1) the more traditional seven-point ideological placement $(\overline{X} = 0.52, M = 0.50$, s.d. $= 0.32)$; (2) the new operational ideology measure, which is constructed as the percentage of policy preferences reported as conservative $(\overline{X} = 0.51, M = 0.50$, s.d. $= 0.34)$;[41] and (3) an index of underlying issue preferences constructed from responses to questions about gun control, abortion, immigration, taxes, healthcare and trade $(\alpha = 0.83; \overline{X} = 0.42, M = 0.42,$ s.d. $= 0.24)$.[42] The correlations between these variables are displayed in Table 12, which also includes partisanship for reference. Note that all of these variables are rescaled to range from 0 to 1, with higher values indicating more conservative/ Republican responses.

Although the two ideology measures are similar, the new operational measure is more representative of respondents' underlying issue preferences. The differences are modest, but the operational measure offers increases over the more traditional measure in all areas. Thus, it appears that asking the ideology question in a different way does improve estimates of underlying issue preferences.

The advantages of the operational measure become more evident when comparing correlations for different types of respondents. First, I look at how correlations vary according to the respondent's political knowledge.[43] Those with lower levels of political knowledge are more likely to be "conflicted" ideologues (Claassen, Tucker, and Smith 2014), and thus, they should be the most impacted by a question that better clarifies which of the two types of ideology is the intended target.

---

[41] Because the sum of the two responses was forced to equal 100, using the percentage reported liberal or the difference of the two does not change the results.

[42] For full question wordings and factor loadings, see the Appendix.

[43] Political knowledge is assessed with the same six questions described in Section 2.1.

Table 12 Correlations between issue preferences and ideological measures, 2018 CES module

	Traditional ideology	Operational ideology	Partisanship
Operational ideology	0.85	–	0.72
Partisanship	0.69	0.72	–
Gun control	0.50	0.52	0.46
Abortion	0.63	0.66	0.60
Immigration	0.62	0.67	0.64
Taxes	0.44	0.47	0.43
Healthcare	0.62	0.63	0.60
Trade	0.49	0.53	0.49
Full index	0.74[a]	0.79	0.72[a]

[a] Different from the operational ideology coefficient at $p < 0.05$.

Second, I look at how correlations vary by strength of partisan attachment. Since both the strength of ideological identity and the consistency of issue preferences increase with partisan extremity (Devine 2015; Levendusky 2010; Westfall et al. 2015), those with stronger party attachments should already have more consistent operational and symbolic ideologies and thus, there should be less room for improvement. Focusing more heavily on operational versus symbolic ideology should also particularly impact pure independents by lessening the emphasis on identity. Many independents actually lean left or right but choose the independent label because they want to avoid associations with labels or parties (Klar and Krupnikov 2016). I expect that when confronted with a traditional ideological self-placement question, many of these independents also are likely to select "moderate" for many of the same reasons.[44] Subsequently, putting the focus more on describing one's political beliefs versus labeling oneself should encourage these types of independents to give responses that are more reflective of their true operational ideology.

As Figures 10 and 11 show, the operational measure does improve correlations as expected. Among those with the lowest two levels of political knowledge, the operational measure results in significantly ($p < 0.05$) stronger correlations. Likewise, the increases observed among pure independents and weak partisans are also significant ($p < 0.05$). Because these are groups that past research shows to

[44] Indeed, in my 2019 Lucid sample, almost 65 percent of independents select the ideological midpoint, and of those, just over 25 percent give a reason that is classified as either "Neither" or "Neutral/Open-Minded."

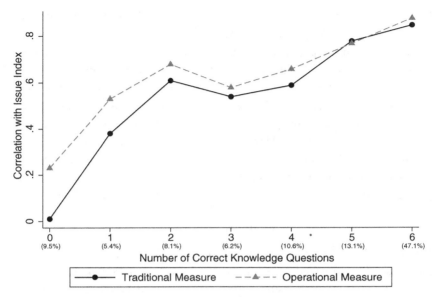

Figure 10 Correlations between ideological measures and issue preferences by political knowledge, 2018 CES

Note: Values in parentheses indicate the percentage of respondents falling into that category.

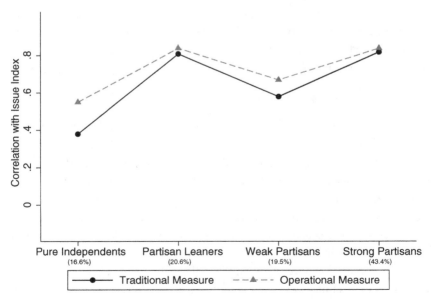

Figure 11 Correlations between ideological measures and issue preferences by partisan attachment, 2018 CES

Note: Values in parentheses indicate the percentage of respondents falling into that category.

be more likely to have conflicting operational and symbolic ideological identifications, this suggests that the improvements of the new operational measure are
related to the more explicit focus of the question. It's also worth noting that the
percentages in Figures 10 and 11 indicate that this is a rather politically engaged
sample; were there more respondents falling into the low knowledge or low partisan
attachment categories, the overall improvement for the full sample would likely be
greater. Thus, the resulting implication is that the general public may be capable of
a higher level of ideological thinking than studies using the traditional measure
usually suggest. My results imply that the lack of correlation between the traditional
question and issue preferences should also be at least partially attributed to confusion related to the question rather than just confusion about or lack of ideology.

3.4 In Summation

Past studies have shown that a large portion of the electorate avoids ideological
labels, and that those who do identify as ideological often do so for reasons that
have nothing to do with issues. Using more recent data and more nuanced
questions, I have shown that ideological thinking is much more prevalent than
previously assumed. Whether thinking about others or themselves, even the
more unaware or unengaged individuals appear able to connect policy beliefs to
ideological terms. A full discussion of the implications that my findings have for
survey research is beyond the scope of my argument. But a key takeaway is that
considering a wider variety of samples and/or approaches suggest an electorate
that is not predominantly innocent or confused. The next step, then, is to show
that this ideological thinking plays an important role in politics.

4 The Importance of Ideology

On Election Night 2020, over 6.3 million (60.8 percent) of Florida's voters
supported raising the state's minimum wage to $15.00 an hour by 2026. The
passage of this ballot measure put Florida on a short but growing list of states that
includes such liberal strongholds as California, Massachusetts, and New York.
And yet at the same time, Florida's voters also awarded the state's twenty-nine
electoral votes to Republican presidential candidate Donald Trump. Similarly,
majorities in Montana and South Dakota voted to liberalize their marijuana laws
while also supporting Trump and Republican candidates for the US Senate. This
type of apparent disconnect between the policies that individuals favor and the
candidates they ultimately vote for contributes to questions about whether issues
really matter. But aside from the obvious problems with inferring individual
behavior from aggregate results, there's also the matter of whether voting based
on the issues necessarily means voting based on *every* issue. As political scientist

Walter Stone (2017) argues, when thinking about voters' decisions, we have to consider the limited options presented to them. Even a somewhat distant copartisan candidate is usually still closer than the candidate from the other side. Minimum wage and marijuana legalization are just two of a host of issues voters must consider and thus, a candidate does not have to be a perfect match in order to be the best match. To be sure, voters in both Florida and Montana also approved more conservative ballot measures, with the former changing the state constitution to explicitly state that voting is limited to US citizens and the latter removing local governments' authorities to regulate the carrying of concealed weapons.

Thus, the results of the 2020 election do not suggest that issues are completely irrelevant, but rather, they illustrate the complexity of disentangling when and how ideological concerns operate alongside partisanship. In the next sections, I draw on both survey and experimental findings to show that ideology does play a role in both voting and affective polarization. By the end of the section, it should be clear that while party tends to reign supreme, ideology is still far from inconsequential.

4.1 Ideology and the Vote

To examine the relationship between ideology and the vote, I follow the standard set by Kinder and Kalmoe (2017) and rely on panel data. Though this approach still does not allow for causal claims, drawing my predictor variables from a survey wave conducted well prior to the wave where respondents were asked about their preferences does aid in trying to parse out which is driving which. That is, this design follows the logic that cause should precede effect.

Using the 2010–2014 CES panel analyzed in Section 2, I examine (1) an individual's 2012 presidential and US House votes as function of their 2010 opinions and characteristics; and (2) an individual's 2014 US House vote as a function of their 2012 opinions and characteristics. I also analyze data from two waves of the VOTER (Views of the Electorate Research) panel study.[45] This panel offers a nationally representative sample of 4,838 US adults who were surveyed between April 5 and May 15, 2018, and then again between November 17, 2018 and January 7, 2019. With these data, I can examine an individual's 2018 US House vote and 2020 presidential vote intention[46] as a function of the opinions and characteristics measured on the early 2018 wave.

---

[45] For details and information on accessing the data, see www.voterstudygroup.org/publication/2019-voter-survey-full-data-set.

[46] Since the Democratic nominee was not yet determined, this was a more generic question about a preference for Trump versus a Democratic candidate.

In all cases, I focus only on those expressing a preference for one of the two major party candidates and code the dependent variable as 1 if the person prefers the Republican candidate and 0 if the person prefers the Democratic candidate. Partisanship is derived from individuals' self-placements on the seven-point scale during the earlier wave of the panel. I represent ideology in two ways: individuals' early wave self-placements[47] and an index of individuals' early wave issue opinions.[48] These two measures should capture both the symbolic and operational aspects of ideology. But while they may be conceptually distinct, they are highly correlated ($r = 0.82$ in the 2010 CES; $r = 0.83$ in the 2012 CES; $r = 0.66$ in the May 2018 VOTER survey) and difficult to disentangle when using survey data. So to give the most accurate view of how ideology in either form may operate alongside partisanship, I run four models for each of my dependent variables: one that includes partisanship but omits both ideology measures, one that includes partisanship and ideological identification, one that includes partisanship and issue opinions (i.e., operational ideology), and one that includes all three.

The full results of these models – which include survey weights and controls for opinions on the nation's economy and individual demographics – are available in the Appendix. Table 13 shows just the key coefficients.

The results in Table 13 show that although partisanship is always a strong predictor of preferences, ideology also plays an important role. The coefficients for both ideological identification and issue preferences retain statistical significance even in the full models. This is particularly notable when looking at preferences for the US House, as this clearly contradicts Kinder and Kalmoe's (2017) conclusion that "ideological voting appears to be negligible, or nearly so, in elections for Congress" (p. 100). In the three House elections examined here, ideology appears to play a substantial role.

To more clearly show this added value of ideology, I run models that interact the two ideology variables with indicators for the respondent's partisan identification.[49] Figures 12 and 13 display predicted probabilities derived from these models.[50] In each, the circles represent predictions for those at the 10th percentile of ideology (i.e., the more liberal end of the scale) for that partisan group, while the triangles represent the predictions for those at the 90th percentile of ideology (i.e., the more conservative end of the scale).

---

[47] The CES utilizes a seven-point scale, while the VOTER panel uses a five-point scale.

[48] The CES issues are the same as those used in Section 2. The VOTER issue questions cover opinions on immigration, taxes, marijuana, North Korea, hate speech, and flag burning. See the Appendix for full question wording. When multiple questions are asked about an issue, I construct an issue index prior to including in the full index.

[49] I create two indicators: one for strong, weak, and leaning Democrats, and one for strong, weak, and leaning Republicans. This leaves pure independents as the omitted baseline.

[50] Full results are available in the Appendix.

Table 13 Estimated effects of partisanship and ideology on voting

2012 presidential vote, 2010–2012 CES panel			
Partisanship	6.88^a (0.44)	5.31^a (0.40)	5.08^a (0.45)	4.71^a (0.41)
Ideological identification		5.70^a (0.48)		3.46^a (0.71)
Issue index			8.50^a (0.97)	6.71^a (1.16)

2012 US House vote, 2010–2012 CES panel			
Partisanship	5.46^a (0.34)	4.21^a (0.33)	3.78^a (0.34)	3.67^a (0.34)
Ideological identification		3.81^a (0.47)		1.83^a (0.55)
Issue index			6.39^a (0.63)	5.03^a (0.65)

2014 US House vote, 2012–2014 CES panel			
Partisanship	5.21^a (0.30)	3.69^a (0.37)	3.77^a (0.31)	3.29^a (0.38)
Ideological identification		3.77^a (0.61)		1.90^a (0.77)
Issue index			6.79^a (0.46)	4.63^a (0.59)

2018 US House vote, 2018–2019 VOTER panel			
	8.42^a (0.47)	6.96^a (0.46)	6.87^a (0.46)	6.27^a (0.47)
		4.04^a (0.67)		2.25^a (0.74)
			5.99^a (0.62)	5.11^a (0.66)

2020 presidential vote intention, 2018–2019 VOTER panel			
Partisanship	8.08^a (0.53)	6.59^a (0.54)	6.53^a (0.53)	5.92^a (0.53)
Ideological identification		4.91^a (0.57)		2.66^a (.67)
Issue index			9.48^a (0.73)	8.81^a (0.84)

Note: Entries are logistic regression coefficients with standard errors in parentheses. Dependent variables are drawn from the later waves of the surveys and coded 1 if the individual preferred the Republican, 0 if they preferred the Democrat. All independent variables are drawn from the earlier waves of the surveys. Partisanship, ideology, and issues are coded to range from 0 to 1 so that higher values indicate more Republican/conservative positions. Full model results that include additional controls are available in the Appendix.
[a] $p < 0.05$.

As should be expected, the effects of ideology are most apparent when looking at pure independents. Among these individuals, a shift from more liberal to more conservative identification or a shift from more liberal to more conservative beliefs moves the predicted probability of preferring the Republican from below 50 percent to above 50 percent. This is particularly true when looking at the issue index measure of ideology, where all effects are statistically significant ($p < 0.05$).[51] Having more conservative issue preferences versus more liberal

---

[51] In contrast, the coefficients for ideological identification are only significant ($p < 0.05$) in the 2018 U.S. House vote and 2020 presidential vote intention models.

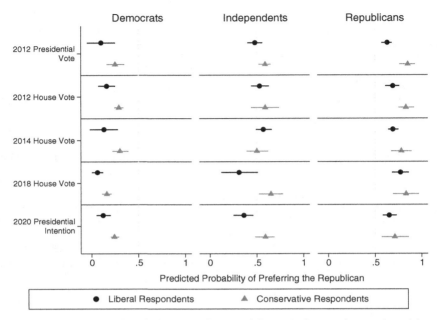

Figure 12 Predicted probabilities of a Republican preference by partisanship
and ideological identification

Note: Estimates derived from models shown in the Appendix. Bars represent the
95 percent confidence intervals.

issue preferences increases the probability of preferring the Republican by
anywhere from 0.39 (2018 US House vote) to 0.66 (2012 presidential vote).

The effects seem weaker when looking at partisans, but only one of the
interactions between the partisanship indicators and the issue index is not
significant.[52] Across all models, the average predicted increase in the probability
of preferring the Republican that results from a shift from more liberal to more
conservative policy preferences is about 0.21. And importantly, these effects are
not limited to just the most politically knowledgeable respondents. Figure 14 plots
the marginal effects of the issue index on the 2014 US House vote for respondents
at all levels of political knowledge.[53] Again, despite expectations of low levels of
ideological voting in these typically less salient elections (e.g. Kinder and Kalmoe
2017), Figure 14 shows that even those at the lowest levels of political knowledge

---

[52] The relationship between the issue index and 2014 U.S. House vote is significantly ($p < 0.05$)
   smaller for Democrats versus pure independents.

[53] I am only able to test for these conditional effects with the CES panel, as the VOTER panel does
   not feature an objective knowledge battery. Models for all three key outcomes are available in the
   Appendix. For parsimony, I only present the results of the 2014 U.S. House vote here in the main
   text.

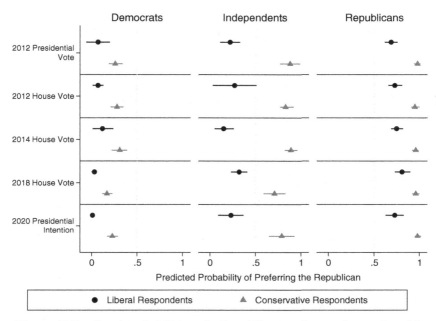

Figure 13 Predicted probabilities of a Republican preference by partisanship and issue preferences

Note: Estimates derived from models shown in the Appendix. Bars represent the 95 percent confidence intervals.

can and do connect their issue preferences to their vote choice. Overall, then, it is clear that ideology, and in particular, operational ideology, allows for substantively important differentiation between individuals who share the same party label.

4.2 Ideology and Affect

As noted in Section 1, there is a growing body of research showing that actual policy positions do in fact play a role in fueling conflict. None of these studies, however, fully address the possibility that these issue effects may just be a product of ideological identity and not preferences. Rogowski and Sutherland (2016) use ideological labels but not issue positions. Webster and Abramowitz (2017) include both, but manipulate them concurrently. The remaining works (Clifford 2020; Lelkes 2021; Orr and Huber 2020) do not include or manipulate ideological labels in their experimental treatments; they only use issue positions. Without an experimental design that explicitly accounts for these two distinct aspects of ideology, we cannot rule out the possibility that the observed issue effects are driven by people's assumption of the corresponding ideological identity. That is, it may be the case that an individual harbors negative feelings toward another person not because

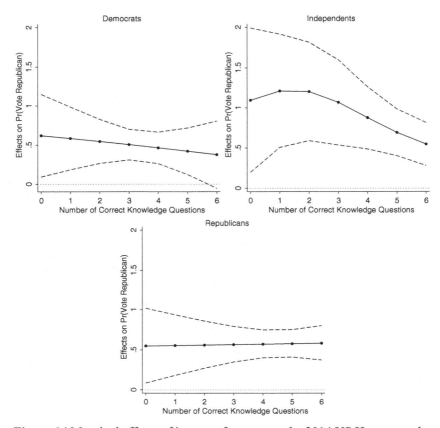

Figure 14 Marginal effects of issue preferences on the 2014 US House vote by partisanship and political knowledge, 2014 CES

Note: Estimates derived from a model shown in the Appendix. Points represent the marginal effects of the issue index, while dashed lines represent the 95 percent confidence intervals.

they take a pro-life stance, but rather, because a pro-life stance signals a conservative group affiliation. As such, I present two survey experiments that allow me to better assess how ideological identity and issue positions each impact partisan polarization.

4.2.1 Experimental Design

Both experiments were administered as part of my 2019 Lucid survey. The sample sizes in the following analyses are reduced because I focus on just the subset of treatments that allow for the clearest illustration of how ideological labels and issue positions augment the role that the party labels

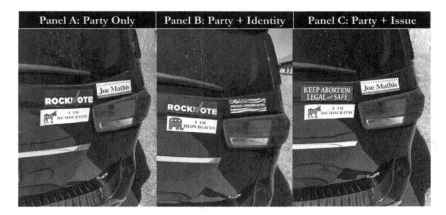

Figure 15 Examples of the bumper sticker treatments
Note: The cues in all treatments were consistent with what would be expected given full partisan sorting.

play in fueling animosity. That is, I focus on strong, weak, and leaning Democrats who received Republican treatments, and strong, weak, or leaning Republicans who received Democratic treatments.[54] This, combined with the fact that I show only the results of the most relevant treatments, reduces my subject pools to 348 in the bumper sticker experiment and 321 in the candidate website experiment.

Like Orr and Huber (2020), my first experiment gauged affect toward an ordinary member of the general public. Each subject was randomly exposed to one of three pictures of a car displaying three political bumper stickers. In the *Party Only* condition (Panel A of Figure 15), one bumper sticker signaled partisanship (Democrat or Republican), while the other two featured generic political message that did signal partisanship or either type of ideology. In the *Party + Identity* condition (Panel B of Figure 15), one bumper sticker signaled party identification, one bumper sticker signaled ideological identification (liberal or conservative), and the third was generic. In the *Party + Issue* condition (Panel C of Figure 15), one bumper sticker signaled party identification, one bumper sticker signaled an issue position (pro-choice or pro-life), and the third was generic. Combinations were constructed to be consistent with partisan sorting such that subjects never received conflicting cues (e.g. a liberal Republican or a pro-life Democrat). Note also that all treatments featured the same number of bumper stickers that all contained some type of political content to account for the facts that many individuals are turned off

---

[54] Analyses testing for differences between Democratic and Republican subjects are available in the Appendix.

Figure 16 Examples of the website treatments
Note: The cues in all treatments were consistent with what would be expected given full partisan sorting.

by political expressions, regardless of content (Klar and Krupnikov 2016; Klar, Krupnikov, and Ryan 2018), and estimates of affective polarization may be inflated by assumptions about the frequency of such expressions (Druckman et al. 2022). Thus, any differences between the treatments should reflect reactions to the messages on the bumper stickers and not just reactions to their presence and quantity.

Following exposure, subjects were asked to use a five-point scale to indicate how upset they would be if the driver of the vehicle pictured moved in next door to them, married a member of their family, or was hired as their new coworker. Responses are averaged ($\alpha = 0.91$)[55] and rescaled to create a measure of social distance that ranges from 0 to 1 ($\overline{X} = 0.31$; s.d. $= 0.28$). They were then asked to use a 0–100 scale to rate the overall favorability of the driver. When also rescaled to range from 0 to 1, this measure has a mean of 0.46 and a standard deviation of 0.25.

To test whether identities and issues have similar effects on evaluations of political elites,[56] I conducted a second experiment where subjects were asked to share the opinions they formed after viewing a candidate webpage. Though the candidate featured – Joseph King – was fictitious, Figure 16 shows that the treatments were designed to look like a real (albeit amateur) campaign homepage. Like the bumper sticker experiment, the candidate website experiment featured three conditions that either signaled just party identification (Panel A of Figure 16), or signaled party plus either ideological identity or issues (Panels B and C of Figure 16).

After viewing the website and responding to three distractor questions, subjects answered a series of questions that are used to construct two dependent variables of interest. First, subjects were asked to use a 100-point scale to rate the favorability of candidate King. When rescaled to range from 0 to 1, this candidate favorability measure has a mean of 0.38 and a standard deviation of 0.27.

---

[55] Statistics reported for the analytical sample.
[56] This approach is also more akin to that of Rogowski and Sutherland (2016), Webster and Abramowitz (2017), and Lelkes (2021).

Next, subjects were asked to use a five-point scale to indicate how likely they would be to engage in four types of political activity: voting for King, displaying a sign, sticker or button for King, donating to King's campaign, and supporting King's opponent. The last item is reverse coded and all four are averaged to form a positive participation index ($\alpha = 0.83$) that is rescaled to range from 0 to 1 ($\overline{X} = 0.33$; s.d. $= 0.22$).

4.2.2 Experimental Results

Table 14 shows the mean values for each treatment group. By comparing each of the party + treatments back to the party only treatment, I will be able to see if/how the extra cue impacts polarization above and beyond the effects of just party alone. Additionally, comparing the ideological identity to the issue treatments will allow me to see if/how the effect of the two types of cues differ.

Across all four variables, the *Party + Issue* treatments lead to the greatest amount of polarization. However, the differences between the treatments are not statistically significant for either of the favorability variables. But. when looking at support for the candidate featured on the website, the *Party + Issue* treatment is significantly different ($p < 0.05$) from the *Party + Identity* treatment. This suggests that while neither significantly increases the negative feelings created by the party label alone, operational ideology still appears to contribute to animosity in a way that ideological identity does not.[57]

This is also the case when looking at social distance from the driver with political bumper stickers. Moreover, the addition of the issue bumper sticker produces a significantly greater desire for social distance that just the partisan bumper sticker alone. This holds even if I deconstruct the social distance index and analyze each questions individually. These findings not only reinforce the work of Orr and Huber (2020), but advance it, as they speak to critiques that those prior findings of an issue effect were simply driven by the inferred ideological identity. Thus, while the results are not consistent across all of the variables that I examine, my experimental work still evidences the argument that issues do play a role in some aspects of polarization.

---

[57] In the Appendix, I present analyses that suggest that this is not just because the ideological label is not too highly correlated with partisan label to have a meaningful impact. Following the questions used to construct my dependent variables, I also asked respondents to predict whether the driver or the candidate would be for or against an issue that was not featured in any of the treatments. In the bumper sticker experiment, the issue was expansion of government healthcare, and in the website experiment, the issue was free college. In both experiments, respondents in the *Party + Identity* treatments were less likely to select "don't know/not enough information" than those who only saw the party cue. Though this difference is only statistically significant ($p < 0.02$) in the website experiment, This suggests that individuals did infer additional information from the ideological cue, but that those inferences did not lead to an increase in animosity.

Table 14 Polarization by treatment group, 2019 Lucid sample

Bumper sticker experiment

	Social distance	Favorability
Party Only	0.27 (0.27)	0.45 (0.24)
	$N = 121$	$N = 121$
Party + Identity	0.27 (0.26)	0.47 (0.23)
	$N = 115$	$N = 113$
Party + Issue	0.38[a, b] (.30)	0.44 (0.27)
	$N = 108$	$N = 108$

Website experiment

	Favorability	Support
Party Only	0.40 (0.27)	0.33 (0.21)
	$N = 85$	$N = 88$
Party + Identity	0.40 (0.26)	0.36 (0.20)
	$N = 109$	$N = 109$
Party + Issue	0.35 (0.29)	0.29[b] (0.23)
	$N = 120$	$N = 122$

Note: Cell entries are group means with standard deviations in parentheses.
[a] Different from Party Only at $p < 0.05$.
[b] Different from Party + Identity at $p < 0.05$.

And importantly, analyses in the Appendix show that the addition of issue information did not also significantly increase animosity when the hypothetical driver or candidate was from the respondent's own party. In fact, the addition of issue information significantly ($p < 0.04$) increased the favorability of the candidate when compared to both other treatments. This suggests that what I am finding is not just a more general aversion for issue-specific political conversation from either side (Druckman et al. 2022; Klar, Krupnikov, and Ryan 2018), and that at least when judging co-partisan elites, issue information may make an individual more appealing. So while more needs to be done to probe some of the inconsistencies in my findings, these results still push back against claims that operational ideology does not play a role in polarization and adds to growing evidence that there is a more substantive basis to the disdain shown for partisan opponents.

4.3 In Summation

Though Americans often appear to support or oppose a political side in much the same way that they cheer for or against a football team, the evidence presented in this section shows that issue opinions do play an important role in the way people vote and the feelings they harbor for the other side. While partisanship is a major predictor of vote choice, my models show that ideology, particularly operational ideology, also serves an important role and reveals differences in the behavior of individuals with the same party identification. Also of note is the fact that my experiments separate the effects of the issue and identity aspects of ideology, showing that the former has effects distinct from the latter. Together, the results shown in this section refute the idea that ideology is nothing more than an identity. Yet this evidence also raises questions about the consequences of increased ideological thinking in the electorate. And thus, I explore these and other implications in my concluding remarks.

5 Not That Innocent

In a reflection on his earlier work, Converse (2006) himself acknowledged that his "portrait of the policy perceptions of the 1960s was subject to easily discriminable change due to the nature of the times" (p. 305). Though a quick glance through any modern social media feed may suggest that change in the levels of political ignorance has not yet occurred, the evidence presented in this Element says otherwise. My look at more updated survey data shows that even the least informed individuals display levels of opinion consistency and stability that surpass that of the more informed individuals analyzed prior to 2010. My examination of open-ended responses and an alternative question format shows that most people can and do connect ideological labels to policy and general philosophy. And finally, my analyses of voting preferences and partisan affect show that operational ideology is an important factor to consider when looking at the behaviors and attitudes of the modern American electorate. So while there are still many Americans who are best classified as ideologically innocent (again, see social media), my main argument is that this group makes up a much smaller proportion of the overall electorate than both scholars and pundits too often imply.

But to clarify, I do not see myself as offering the last word on this issue. Rather, I see this Element as another, much-needed piece of what should be a lively and ongoing debate. A key contention of Converse's (1964) theory is that the transmission of ideology is a top-down process.[58] Thus, as elites change and evolve over time, it seems imperative to also test for corresponding changes among the public. Moreover, there are a number of other aspects of ideology and ideological thinking that need more attention. For example, I, like a great deal of others working in this area, have focused only on "static"

---

[58] Such a contention is also supported by more recent works showing the influence of elite ideology.

constraint, which is the more specific term for the correlations between issue opinions. This approach seemingly ignores "dynamic" constraint, which can be thought of as the extent to which a change in one opinion leads to a change in a related opinion. But as Coppock and Green (2022) show, the two are distinct, and possession of one type of constraint does not imply the possession of the other. As such, there is still much to be explored to maintain the fullest and most up-to-date understanding of the nature of ideology in the American electorate.

In addition, there are at least two major questions that need to be considered as research progresses. First, exactly what is the standard for classifying an individual or the public at large as "ideological"? Using respondents' volunteered descriptions of politics, Converse (1964) estimated that only about 2.5–3.0 percent of the general public could be classified as ideological. In contrast, more recent analyses of close-ended policy questions from over 285,000 respondents conclude that only about one in five Americans should be classified as "Conversian,"[59] while about seven in ten Americans "have preferences across policy questions that are well approximated by an ideal point on an underlying liberal–conservative ideological dimension" (Fowler et al. 2022, p. 4). My analyses offer a variety of estimates that fall between these two. But what is consistent across methods and measures is that political knowledge plays an important role. So regardless of the threshold one applies, ideologues should predominantly come from the highest strata of knowledge and subsequently, only be a subset of the overall population. And thus, the continued debate should not be focused on *if* the public is ideological, but rather, *what portion* of the population is ideological and how different degrees of ideological thinking impact our political processes.

Second, is an ideological public actually desirable? Though I title this project a defense, I do not make claims about the more normative implications. On the one hand, a lack of ideological thinking is often equated with a lack of information and could hinder the public's ability to hold representatives accountable for their choices. As summed up by Tomz and Sniderman (2005), "a lack of constraint – an inability to connect positions across issues – would raise deep problems for democracy. It would signify not only the limited competence of individuals to understand politics, but also a fundamental absence of shared understanding about political programs ... Under these conditions, it is not obvious what electoral representation can mean" (p. 1). Yet, the decisions made by those lacking constraint should not automatically be

---

[59] The authors define a Conversian as someone who "expresses policy views that are neither well described by a single left–right ideological dimension nor best classified as random" (Fowler et al. 2022, p. 11).

assumed irrational. In the absence of ideological thinking, voters shift their focus to "highly relevant character themes, such as the candidate's perceived competence, integrity and leadership qualities" which then provide "ideological and non-ideological voters the tools to appraise presidential candidates meaningfully and make informed choices" (Lavine and Gschwend 2007, p. 160). Even more, to the extent that ideological constraint stems from desires to conform with social norms, then the elites who shape those norms will have substantial power to influence the preferences of even the most politically knowledgeable voters (Groenendyk, Kimbrough, and Pickup 2022; Sartori 1969). Thus, the continuation of these debates about both the actual and ideal levels of ideological constraint in the mass public are crucial to gaining greater insights into the (dis)functioning of American democracy.

References

Abramowitz, Alan I. 2011. *The Disappearing Center: Engaged Citizens, Polarization, and American Democracy*. New Haven: Yale University Press.

Achen, Christopher H. 1975. "Mass Political Attitudes and the Survey Response." *American Political Science Review* 69(4): 1218–31.

Aldrich, John H., and Richard D. Mckelvey. 1977. "A Method of Scaling with Applications to the 1968 and 1972 Presidential Elections." *American Political Science Review* 71(1): 111–30.

Aldrich, John H., Richard G. Niemi, George Rabinowitz, and David W. Rohde. 1982. "The Measurement of Public Opinion about Public Policy: A Report on Some New Issue Question Formats." *American Journal of Political Science* 26(2): 391–414.

Ansolabehere, Stephen, and Douglas Rivers. 2013. "Cooperative Survey Research." *Annual Review of Political Science* 16: 307–29.

Ansolabehere, Stephen, Jonathan Rodden, and James M. Snyder. 2008. "The Strength of Issues: Using Multiple Measures to Gauge Preference Stability, Ideological Constraint, and Issue Voting." *American Political Science Review* 102(2): 215–32.

Ansolabehere, Stephen, and Brian F. Schaffner. 2014. "Does Survey Mode Still Matter? Findings from a 2010 Multi-Mode Comparison." *Political Analysis* 22(3): 285–303.

Bankert, Alexa. 2021. "Negative and Positive Partisanship in the 2016 U.S. Presidential Elections." *Political Behavior* 43(4): 1467–85.

Barber, Michael, and Jeremy C. Pope. 2019. "Does Party Trump Ideology? Disentangling Party and Ideology in America." *American Political Science Review* 113(1): 38–54.

Boudreau, Cheryl, and Scott A. Mackenzie. 2014. "Informing the Electorate? How Party Cues and Policy Information Affect Public Opinion about Initiatives." *American Journal of Political Science* 58(1): 48–62.

Bullock, John G. 2011. "Elite Influence on Public Opinion in an Informed Electorate." *American Political Science Review* 105(3): 496–515.

Canes-Wrone, Brandice, David W. Brady, and John F. Cogan. 2002. "Out of Step, Out of Office: Electoral Accountability and House Members' Voting." *American Political Science Review* 96(1): 127–40.

Chang, Linchiat, and Jon A. Krosnick. 2009. "National Surveys via RDD Telephone Interviewing versus the Internet: Comparing Sample

Representativeness and Response Quality." *Public Opinion Quarterly* 73(4): 641–78.

Chong, Dennis, and Kevin J. Mullinix. 2019. "Information and Issue Constraints on Party Cues." *American Politics Research* 47(6): 1209–38.

Claassen, Christopher, Patrick Tucker, and Steven S. Smith. 2014. "Ideological Labels in America." *Political Behavior* 37(2): 253–78.

Clifford, Scott. 2020. "Compassionate Democrats and Tough Republicans: How Ideology Shapes Partisan Stereotypes." *Political Behavior* 42(4): 1269–93.

Clifford, Scott, Ryan M. Jewell, and Philip D. Waggoner. 2015. "Are Samples Drawn from Mechanical Turk Valid for Research on Political Ideology?" *Research and Politics* 2(4).

Collitt, Samuel, and Benjamin Highton. 2021. "The Policy Polarization of Party Activists in the United States." *American Politics Research* 49(4): 386–99.

Converse, Philip. 1964. "The Nature of Belief Systems in Mass Publics." In *Ideology and Discontent*, ed. David Apter. Gelncoe: The Free Press, 206–61.

   2006. "Democratic Theory and Electoral Reality." *Critical Review* 18(1–3): 297–329.

Converse, Philip, and Roy Pierce. 1986. *Political Representation in France*. Cambridge, MA: Harvard University Press.

Coppock, Alexander, and Donald Green. 2022. "Do Belief Systems Exhibit Dynamic Constraint?" *Journal of Politics* 84(2): 725–38.

Coppock, Alexander, and Oliver A. McClellan. 2019. "Validating the Demographic, Political, Psychological, and Experimental Results Obtained from a New Source of Online Survey Respondents." *Research & Politics* 6(1): 205316801882217.

Cortina, Jose M. 1993. "What Is Coefficient Alpha? An Examination of Theory and Applications." *Journal of Applied Psychology* 78(1): 98–104.

Costa, Mia. 2021. "Ideology, Not Affect: What Americans Want from Political Representation." *American Journal of Political Science* 65(2): 342–58.

Devine, Christopher J. 2015. "Ideological Social Identity: Psychological Attachment to Ideological In-Groups as a Political Phenomenon and a Behavioral Influence." *Political Behavior* 37(3): 509–35.

Dias, Nicholas, and Yphtach Lelkes. 2022. "The Nature of Affective Polarization: Disentangling Policy Disagreement from Partisan Identity." *American Journal of Political Science* 66(3): 775–90.

Dillman, Don A., Glenn Phelps, Robert Tortora et al. 2009. "Response Rate and Measurement Differences in Mixed-Mode Surveys Using Mail, Telephone, Interactive Voice Response (IVR) and the Internet." *Social Science Research* 38(1): 1–18.

Druckman, James N. Samara Klar, Yanna Krupnikov, Matthew Levendusky, and John Barry Ryan. 2022. "(Mis-)Estimating Affective Polarization." The Journal of Politics, 84(2):1106–1117.

Ellis, Christopher, and James Stimson. 2012. *The Journal of Politics* 84(2): 1106–17. New York: Cambridge University Press.

Endres, Kyle, D. Sunshine Hillygus, Matthew DeBell, and Shanto Iyengar. 2023. "A Randomized Experiment Evaluating Survey Mode Effects for Video Interviewing." *Political Science Research and Methods* 11(1): 144–59.

Fiorina, Morris P., Samuel J. Abrams, and Jeremy C. Pope. 2011. *Culture War: The Myth of a Polarized America*. 3rd ed. New York: Pearson.

Fowler, Anthony, Seth J. Hill, Jeffrey B. Lewis et al. 2022. "Moderates." *American Political Science Review*: 1–18.

Freeder, Sean, Gabriel S. Lenz, and Shad Turney. 2019. "The Importance of Knowing 'What Goes with What': Reinterpreting the Evidence on Policy Attitude Stability." *Journal of Politics* 81(1): 274–90.

Gerring, John. 1997. "Ideology: A Definitional Analysis." *Political Research Quarterly* 50(4): 957–94.

Goggin, Stephen N., John A. Henderson, and Alexander G. Theodoridis. 2020. "What Goes with Red and Blue? Mapping Partisan and Ideological Associations in the Minds of Voters." *Political Behavior* 42(4): 985–1013.

Gooch, Andrew, and Lynn Vavreck. 2019. "How Face-to-Face Interviews and Cognitive Skill Affect Item Non-Response: A Randomized Experiment Assigning Mode of Interview." *Political Science Research and Methods* 7(1): 143–62.

Groenendyk, Eric, Erik O. Kimbrough, and Mark Pickup. 2022. "How Norms Shape the Nature of Belief Systems in Mass Publics." *American Journal of Political Science*.

Guggenheim, Lauren, Colleen McClain, Yioryos Nardis, and Ted Brader. 2019. *Comparing Face-to-Face and Web Modes in the ANES 2016 Time Series Study*. https://electionstudies.org/wp-content/uploads/2019/09/ANES2016_ModeReport.pdf.

Hare, Christopher, David A. Armstrong, Ryan Bakker, Royce Carroll, and Keith T. Poole. 2015. "Using Bayesian Aldrich-McKelvey Scaling to Study

Citizens' Ideological Preferences and Perceptions." *American Journal of Political Science* 59(3): 759–74.

Hare, Christopher, and Keith T. Poole. 2014. "The Polarization of Contemporary American Politics." *Polity* 46(3): 411–29.

Hetherington, Marc J. 2001. "Resurgent Mass Partisanship: The Role of Elite Polarization." *American Political Science Review* 95(3): 619–31.

Iyengar, Shanto, Gaurav Sood, and Yphtach Lelkes. 2012. "Affect, Not Ideology: A Social Identity Perspective on Polarization." *Public Opinion Quarterly* 76(3): 405–31.

Iyengar, Shanto, and Sean J. Westwood. 2015. "Fear and Loathing across Party Lines: New Evidence on Group Polarization." *American Journal of Political Science* 59(3): 690–707.

Jennings, M. Kent. 1992. "Ideological Thinking among Mass Publics and Political Elites." *Public Opinion Quarterly* 56(4): 419–41.

Joesten, Danielle A., and Walter J. Stone. 2014. "Reassessing Proximity Voting: Expertise, Party, and Choice in Congressional Elections." *Journal of Politics* 76(3): 740–53.

Keith, Bruce E., David B. Magleby, Candice J. Nelson, Elizabeth A. Orr, and Mark C. Westlye. 1992. *The Myth of the Independent Voter*. Berkeley: University of California Press.

Kinder, Donald R., and Nathan P. Kalmoe. 2017. *Neither Liberal or Conservative: Ideological Innocence in the American Public*. Chicago: University of Chicago Press.

Klar, Samara, and Yanna Krupnikov. 2016. *Independent Politics: How American Disdain for Parties Leads to Politica Inaction*. New York: Cambridge University Press.

Klar, Samara, Yanna Krupnikov, and John Barry Ryan. 2018. "Affective Polarization or Partisan Disdain? Untangling a Dislike for the Opposing Party from a Dislike of Partisanship." *Public Opinion Quarterly* 82(2): 379–90.

Krosnick, Jon A. 1991. "Response Strategies for Coping with the Cognitive Demands of Attitude Measures in Surveys." *Applied Cognitive Psychology* 5(3): 213–36.

Krosnick, Jon A., and Matthew K. Berent. 1993. "Comparisons of Party Identification and Policy Preferences: The Impact of Survey Question Format." *American Journal of Political Science* 37(3): 941–64.

Krupnikov, Yanna, and Adam Seth Levine. 2014. "Cross-Sample Comparisons and External Validity." *Journal of Experimental Political Science* 1(1): 59–80.

Lavine, Howard, and Thomas Gschwend. 2007. "Issues, Party and Character: The Moderating Role of Ideological Thinking on Candidate Evaluation." *British Journal of Political Science* 37(1): 139–63.

Lelkes, Yphtach. 2021. "Policy over Party: Comparing the Effects of Candidate Ideology and Party on Affective Polarization." *Political Science Research and Methods* 9(1): 189–96.

Lelkes, Yphtach, and Sean J. Westwood. 2017. "The Limits of Partisan Prejudice." *Journal of Politics* 79(2): 485–501.

Lenz, Gabriel S. 2012. *Follow the Leader? How Voters Respond to Politicians' Policies and Performance*. Chicago: University of Chicago Press.

Levendusky, Matthew S. 2010. "Clearer Cues, More Consistent Voters: A Benefit of Elite Polarization." *Political Behavior* 32(1): 111–31.

Malhotra, Neil, Jon A. Krosnick, and Randall K. Thomas. 2009. "Optimal Design of Branching Questions to Measure Bipolar Constructs." *Public Opinion Quarterly* 73(2): 304–24.

Malka, Ariel and Yphtach Lelkes. 2010. "More than Ideology: Conservative-Liberal Identity and Receptivity to Political Cues." *Social Justice Research*, 23: 156–188.

Mason, Lilliana. 2018. "Ideologues without Issues: The Polarizing Consequences of Ideological Identities." *Public Opinion Quarterly* 82 (S1): 280–301.

Mullinix, Kevin J. 2016. "Partisanship and Preference Formation: Competing Motivations, Elite Polarization, and Issue Importance." *Political Behavior* 38(2): 383–411.

Mummolo, Jonathan, Erik Peterson, and Sean Westwood. 2019. "The Limits of Partisan Loyalty." *Political Behavior* 43: 949–72.

Nicholson, Stephen P. 2012. "Polarizing Cues." *American Journal of Political Science* 56(1): 52–66.

Orr, Lilla V., and Gregory A. Huber. 2020. "The Policy Basis of Measured Partisan Animosity in the United States." *American Journal of Political Science* 64(3): 569–86.

Ozer, Adam. 2020. "Well, You're the Expert: How Signals of Source Expertise Help Mitigate Partisan Bias." *Journal of Elections, Public Opinion and Parties*.

Peffley, Mark A., and Jon Hurwitz. 1985. "A Hierarchical Model of Attitude Constraint." *American Journal of Political Science* 29(4): 871–90.

Poole, Keith, and Howard Rosenthal. 1997. *Congress: A Political-Economic History of Roll Call Voting*. New York: Oxford University Press.

Popp, Elizabeth, and Thomas J. Rudolph. 2011. "A Tale of Two Ideologies: Explaining Public Support for Economic Interventions." *Journal of Politics* 73(3): 808–20.

Rogowski, Jon C., and Joseph L. Sutherland. 2016. "How Ideology Fuels Affective Polarization." *Political Behavior* 38(2): 485–508.

Sartori, Giovanni. 1969. "Politics, Ideology, and Belief Systems." *American Political Science Review* 63(2): 398–411.

Shor, Boris, and Jon C. Rogowski. 2018. "Ideology and the U.S. Congressional Vote." *Political Science Research and Methods* 6(2): 323–41.

Simas, Elizabeth N. 2013. "Proximity Voting in the 2010 U.S. House Elections." *Electoral Studies* 32(4): 708–17.

2018. "Ideology through the Partisan Lens: Applying Anchoring Vignettes to U.S. Survey Research." *International Journal of Public Opinion Research* 30(3): 343–64.

Smith, Brianna, Scott Clifford, and Jennifer Jerit. 2020. "TRENDS: How Internet Search Undermines the Validity of Political Knowledge Measures." *Political Research Quarterly* 73(1): 141–55.

Stone, Walter J. 2017. *Candidates and Voters: Ideology, Valence, and Representation in U.S. Elections*. New York: Cambridge University Press.

Sturgis, Patrick, Caroline Roberts, and Patten Smith. 2014. "Middle Alternatives Revisited: How the neither/nor Response Acts as a Way of Saying 'I Don't Know'?" *Sociological Methods and Research* 43(1): 15–38.

Tausanovitch, Chris, and Christopher Warshaw. 2018. "Does the Ideological Proximity between Candidates and Voters Affect Voting in U.S. House Elections?" *Political Behavior* 40: 223–45.

Tomz, Michael, and Robert P. van Houweling. 2008. "Candidate Positioning and Voter Choice." *American Political Science Review* 102(3): 303–18.

Tomz, Michael, and Paul Sniderman. 2005. *Brand Names and Organization of Mass Belief System*. https://citeseerx.ist.psu.edu/document?repid=rep1&type=pdf&doi=c751bd7df5019b0b135f2e306391e495ac0ad13a.

Treier, Shawn, and D. Sunshine Hillygus. 2009. "The Nature of Political Ideology in the Contemporary Electorate." *Public Opinion Quarterly* 73 (4): 679–703.

Wand, Jonathan. 2013. "Credible Comparisons Using Interpersonally Incomparable Data: Nonparametric Scales with Anchoring Vignettes." *American Journal of Political Science* 57(1): 249–62.

Webster, Steven W., and Alan I. Abramowitz. 2017. "The Ideological Foundations of Affective Polarization in the U.S. Electorate." *American Politics Research* 45(4): 621–47.

Westfall, Jacob, Leaf Van Boven, John R. Chambers, and Charles M. Judd. 2015. "Perceiving Political Polarization in the United States." *Perspectives on Psychological Science* 10(2): 145–58.

Zaller, John. 1985. *Analysis of Information Items in the 1985 ANES Pilot Study.* https://electionstudies.org/wp-content/uploads/2018/07/nes002261.pdf.

Zingher, Joshua N., and Michael E. Flynn. 2018. "From on High: The Effect of Elite Polarization on Mass Attitudes and Behaviors, 1972–2012." *British Journal of Political Science* 48(1): 23–45.

Cambridge Elements

Political Psychology

Yanna Krupnikov
University of Michigan

Yanna Krupnikov is Professor at University of Michigan. Her research focuses on political psychology and political communication, and considers when political messages are most likely to affect people's behaviors. Her work with Cambridge University Press include *Independent Politics* (2016, co-authored with Samara Klar), *The Increasing Viability of Good News* (2021, with Stuart Soroka) and *The Other Divide* (2022, with John Barry Ryan).

About the Series

Most political events and outcomes are the results of people's decisions. This series delves into the psychology behind these decisions to understand contemporary politics. The publications in the series explain real-world political events by using psychology to understand people's motivations, beliefs and, ultimately, behaviors.

Cambridge Elements ≡

Political Psychology

Elements in the Series

In Defense of Ideology: Reexamining the Role of Ideology in the American Electorate
Elizabeth N. Simas

A full series listing is available at: www.cambridge.org/EPPS

Printed in the United States
by Baker & Taylor Publisher Services